Studying  ama

Palgrave Study Guides

A Handbook of Writing for Engineers   *Joan van Emden*
Authoring a PhD   *Patrick Dunleavy*
Effective Communication for Arts and Humanities Students
   Joan van Emden and Lucinda Becker
Effective Communication for Science and Technology   *Joan van Emden*
How to Manage your Arts, Humanities and Social Science Degree   *Lucinda Becker*
How to Manage your Science and Technology Degree   *Lucinda Becker and David Price*
How to Study Foreign Languages   *Marilyn Lewis*
How to Write Better Essays   *Bryan Greetham*
Key Concepts in Politics   *Andrew Heywood*
Making Sense of Statistics   *Michael Wood*
The Mature Student's Guide to Writing   *Jean Rose*
The Postgraduate Research Handbook   *Gina Wisker*
Professional Writing   *Sky Marsen*
Research Using IT   *Hilary Coombes*
Skills for Success   *Stella Cottrell*
The Student's Guide to Writing   *John Peck and Martin Coyle*
The Study Skills Handbook (second edition)   *Stella Cottrell*
Study Skills for Speakers of English as a Second Language
   Marilyn Lewis and Hayo Reinders
Studying Economics   *Brian Atkinson and Susan Johns*
Studying History (second edition)   *Jeremy Black and Donald M. MacRaild*
Studying Mathematics and its Applications   *Peter Kahn*
Studying Physics   *David Sands*
Studying Psychology   *Andrew Stevenson*
Teaching Study Skills and Supporting Learning   *Stella Cottrell*

Palgrave Study Guides: Literature

General Editors: John Peck and Martin Coyle

How to Begin Studying English Literature (third edition)   *Nicholas Marsh*
How to Study a Jane Austen Novel (second edition)   *Vivien Jones*
How to Study Chaucer (second edition)   *Rob Pope*
How to Study a Charles Dickens Novel   *Keith Selby*
How to Study an E. M. Forster Novel   *Nigel Messenger*
How to Study James Joyce   *John Blades*
How to Study Linguistics (second edition)   *Geoffrey Finch*
How to Study Modern Poetry   *Tony Curtis*
How to Study a Novel (second edition)   *John Peck*
How to Study a Poet (second edition)   *John Peck*
How to Study a Renaissance Play   *Chris Coles*
How to Study Romantic Poetry (second edition)   *Paul O'Flinn*
How to Study a Shakespeare Play (second edition)   *John Peck and Martin Coyle*
How to Study Television   *Keith Selby and Ron Cowdery*
Linguistic Terms and Concepts   *Geoffrey Finch*
Literary Terms and Criticism (third edition)   *John Peck and Martin Coyle*
Practical Criticism   *John Peck and Martin Coyle*
Studying Modern Drama (second edition)   *Kenneth Pickering*

Studying Modern Drama

Second Edition

Kenneth Pickering

First edition 1988
Reprinted 7 times
Second edition 2003

Published by
PALGRAVE MACMILLAN
Houndmills, Basingstoke, Hampshire RG21 6XS and
175 Fifth Avenue, New York, N.Y. 10010
Companies and representatives throughout the world

PALGRAVE MACMILLAN is the global academic imprint of the Palgrave Macmillan division of St. Martin's Press, LLC and of Palgrave Macmillan Ltd. Macmillan® is a registered trademark in the United States, United Kingdom and other countries. Palgrave is a registered trademark in the European Union and other countries.

ISBN 1–4039–0441–3

This book is printed on paper suitable for recycling and made from fully managed and sustained forest sources.

10 9 8 7 6 5 4 3 2 1
12 11 10 09 08 07 06 05 04 03

Printed and bound in Great Britain by
Creative Print & Design (Wales), Ebbw vale

For Susannah and Simon

Contents

General Editors' Preface

Everybody who studies literature, either for an examination or simply for pleasure, experiences the same problem: how to understand and respond to the text. As every student of literature knows, it is perfectly possible to read a book over and over again and yet still feel baffled and at a loss as to what to say about it. One answer to this problem, of course, is to accept someone else's view of the text, but how much more rewarding it would be if you could work out your own critical response to any book you choose or are required to study.

The aim of the literature titles in this series is to help you develop your critical skills by offering practical advice about how to read, understand and analyse literary texts. Each volume provides you with a clear method of study so that you can see how to set about tackling texts on your own. While the authors of each volume approach the problem in a different way, every book in the series attempts to provide you with some broad ideas about the kind of texts you are likely to be studying and some broad ideas about how to think about literature; each volume then shows you how to apply these ideas in a way which should help you construct your own analysis and interpretation. Unlike most critical books, therefore, the books in this series do not simply convey someone else's thinking about a text, but encourage you and show you how to think about a text for yourself.

Each book is written with an awareness that you are likely to be preparing for an examination, and therefore practical advice is given not only on how to understand and analyse literature, but also on how to organize a written response. Our hope is that although these books are intended to serve a practical purpose, they may also enrich your enjoyment of literature by making you a more confident reader, alert to the interest and pleasure to be derived from literary texts.

John Peck
Martin Coyle

Acknowledgements

The author wishes to express grateful thanks to Kevin Wood and the cast of Channel Theatre's production of *The Birthday Party* for many new insights; to Irene Pickering for her inexhaustible patience in preparing the manuscript; to Martin Coyle and Suzannah Burywood for their support and helpful suggestions; and to generations of teachers and students.

The author and publishers gratefully acknowledge permission to use copyright material granted by the following: The Random House Group Limited for an extract from *Chips with Everything* by Arnold Wesker, published by Jonathan Cape; Methuen Publishing Ltd for extracts from *A Doll's House* and *Ghosts* by Henrik Ibsen, *Ghost Sonata* by August Strindberg, *Fen* by Caryl Churchill and *Mother Courage and her Children* by Berthold Brecht; Faber & Faber Ltd for extracts from *Mules* by Winsome Pinnock and *The Caretaker* by Harold Pinter; Judy Daish Associates for an extract from *Pack of Lies* by Hugh Whitemore; Casarotto Ramsay & Associates Limited for an extract from *The Glass Menagerie* by Tennessee Williams, copyright © 1945 renewed 1973 by the University of the South, published by New Directions, reprinted by permission of The University of the South, Sewanee, Tennessee; International Creative Management Inc. for an extract from *Death of a Salesman*, copyright © 1949 by Arthur Miller.

All rights whatsoever in all these plays are strictly reserved, and application for performance, etc., must be made before rehearsal to the appropriate agents or publishers as follows: *Chips with Everything*, The Random House Group Ltd, 20 Vauxhall Bridge Road, London, SW1V 2SA; *A Doll's House*, *Ghosts*, *Ghost Sonata* or *Fen*, Methuen Publishing Ltd, 215 Vauxhall Bridge Road, London, SW1V 1EJ; *Mother Courage and her Children*, Samuel French Ltd, 52 Fitzroy St, Fitzrovia, London, W1T 5JR; *Mules* and *The Caretaker*, Faber & Faber Ltd, 3 Queen's Square, London, WC1N 3AU; *A Pack of Lies*, Judy Daish Associates, 2 St Charles St, London, W10 6EG; *The Glass Menagerie*, Casarotto Ramsay & Associates Ltd, National House, 60–66 Wardour St, London, W1V 4ND; and *Death of a Salesman*, International Creative Management Inc., 40 57th Street, New York, NY 10019.

Kenneth Pickering

1 Introduction

▶ Using this book

The purpose of this book is to enable you to make a really good job of responding to any modern play that you might encounter as part of a course. Students are often uneasy about studying modern plays, either because they are baffled as to what the play is about or because they have either read or seen a play, enjoyed it, but simply cannot think what to say about it when it comes to analysis. So, the prospect of writing an essay or examination answer inevitably seems daunting.

I should certainly not be writing the second edition of this book to help you if I did not believe that studying modern plays *can* and *should* be one of the most rewarding experiences in the whole field of drama and literature; but I must admit that there are two reasons why this might not appear to be the case. First, some modern plays seem utterly incomprehensible when you initially encounter them, and you should never be ashamed to admit this to yourself. And don't be discouraged: plenty of sophisticated audiences and critics have at first been totally perplexed by plays that have later established themselves as classics. We must never forget that one of the many options open to a playwright *is* to mystify the audience. Second, drama now enters our homes constantly through television and we are much more likely to consume modern drama than we are novels, poetry or earlier plays. Watching so many 'real life' dramas, soaps, domestic comedies and documentaries makes it difficult for us to conceive of 'studying' an art form we take so much for granted.

How, then *do* we study modern plays, and how can this book be of help? Initially, I am going to ask you to consider five questions before going on to suggest a number of steps to follow in studying a modern play. You will need to think about the five questions very carefully because they provide the basis of our future exploration. You may wish to go on to work your way through all the parts of this book in sequence, but you will notice that at the end of each chapter there is a checklist of things you should have understood and some suggestions for *workshop activities*. Another way of using this book is to turn straight to Chapter 4 entitled 'Practical Workshops for Drama Study' once you have finished reading this introduction and then apply what you have learnt there to the rest of the book. This might be particularly helpful if you are working with a group.

As you acquire new skills and insights from following the steps I suggest you should find yourself able to go deeper into a play and you will grow in confidence as you discover that you are able to make valuable judgements about the material. I am particularly keen that you should come to 'make sense' of what is really the strange and remarkable ritual that we know as 'theatre': a group of people, with you amongst them, sits in a darkened room or in some agreed space and watches another group of people perform. The first group of people, *the audience*, never invades the space of the second group of people, *the performers*. The audience does not usually shout out when they are angry, bored, mystified or can see something that the performers appear not to see. Indeed, they allow the performers to insult them, shock them, amuse them and manipulate their perception in a whole variety of ways. The audience may agree to imagine that a structure on stage is a room in someone's house or that a bare stage represents the universe, or that half an hour represents several hours. The performers may speak directly to the audience or appear to pretend that the audience does not exist. This ritual becomes stranger the more you think about it and we shall return to this description several times in our study. Modern plays are the products of what playwrights have believed to be the appropriate forms of this ritual in recent years. And this leads us to our five questions:

- What is a playtext?
- How do we 'study' modern drama?
- What *is* 'modern drama'?
- What are stage conventions?
- What about film and TV?

▶ What is a playtext?

Almost all the plays you may be required to study will have survived because they have been published in printed form: so students usually start their study by reading the playtext. It is true that, in the contemporary theatre, there are some plays in which the written text is a comparatively small element and we shall be considering this type of 'physical theatre' at a later stage. However, I am going to assume that you are expecting to gain a great deal of understanding by studying a text. When you do this you must be constantly aware that a 'play' as a play really only exists when it is performed. The text is a blueprint for action – a complex set of instructions to the performers. To make this clear, modern Performance Studies tend to refer to the original text as 'the work' so that we understand that the text itself becomes open to an almost infinite number of interpretations. Because the bulk of a playtext consists of the words that the actors must speak, and because these words are chosen and shaped with great skill by the playwright, the playtext itself is often mistakenly thought to be simply another literary form like the novel or poetry. It is not surprising, therefore, that some students find plays difficult to understand, since they have not grasped that the 'meaning' of a play only emerges in the theatre.

The implication of all this is that in studying a play you must recognise that the words spoken by the characters are only one element of a play, and I shall be suggesting ways in which you can interpret the various other indications for performance contained in a playtext. It is even more important for you to remember that as you study a play you will need to construct an imaginary performance in your mind. This may cause you some problems if you have a very limited experience of the theatre, but, once again, there are suggested activities in this book that will help you to overcome this factor. Ideally, you will need to see the play you are studying performed as often as possible, but this may not be easy and you may well experience a sharp clash between the imaginary performance you have constructed in your mind and a live performance you may see. This, in fact, is part of the enjoyment of studying modern drama and you can well imagine how dull it would be if all performances were similar.

In the modern theatre the majority of successful playwrights have been and continue to be deeply involved in the performance of their plays and, as we shall see, this is a period of bold experimentation and considerable change. Playwrights convey many of their wishes and attitudes concerning the performance of their plays in the published playtexts, so when you begin reading a play (and this can be a very enjoyable activity in its own right) remember you are not studying a novel.

▶ How do we study modern drama?

We can study drama in many ways: by reading and analysis, by visiting the theatre, taking part in workshops, writing reflective journals and engaging with the text at a variety of levels. Some of our learning will be conscious and structured and some of it experiential. You have probably obtained this book because you are a student required to study plays, but remember that you are not the only kind of person who needs to do this. If plays were written for performance, then it follows that those who have to be involved in performing them – actors, directors, designers – need to study them with as much perception, care and imagination as students. These practitioners must ask the same crucial question as students of every playtext they encounter: 'How are the playwright's intentions to be realised in performance?'

Students can learn a great deal from the way in which actors and directors approach the study of a play and you will benefit from tackling a play *as if* the end product was a production rather than an essay. Some of the suggestions in this book might provide insights into doing this. The idea of 'study' is usually associated with reading, solitary contemplation and quiet reflection, all of which is valuable. But in the case of drama there are other dimensions. This is why I have included a chapter on workshop approaches to the study of drama and have suggested various practical activities to complement and enrich your study. There is no division between activity and thinking: on the contrary, there is a clearly established link between thought and action, so do not be surprised if you only come to understand a line of a play when you have to speak it for yourself or if you only realise the impact of the entrance of a character into a room when you have experienced it in performance.

Do not be put off by the idea of performance. The aim of this book is not to make you into an actor, and there *will* be a strong emphasis on traditional, bookish study. However, the *possibility* of performance must always be in your mind and I have included various practical activities that are helpful without demanding a high level of acting skill.

▶ What is modern drama?

The precise meaning of the term 'modern' varies according to its context. Rather surprisingly, perhaps, we usually describe as modern any play written since 1877! In this particular year the great Norwegian dramatist Henrik Ibsen turned from writing verse plays to create a series of plays in everyday language dealing with important social and moral issues. It was the impact of these and similar plays on the European Theatre of the late nineteenth century and the rapid spread of their influence to Britain, Russia and the United States of America that began the era of 'modern drama'.

The style of Ibsen's plays is frequently labelled 'naturalistic', and while there have been many departures from naturalism in the modern age, it has remained the dominant mode and, for most of us, the most accessible form of theatre. Television has only strengthened the whole of naturalism. Though we shall return to the idea many times, it is important to note here that we generally *expect* a play to be naturalistic: that is, to show us believable people living credible lives and speaking like ourselves. Because naturalistic plays are the most straightforward to deal with, most of my early examples will be drawn from this kind of play.

Before we leave the question of what is meant by 'modern drama' we must consider some of the factors which modern plays have in common. There are four in particular which are helpful for us to consider here:

First, modern plays are all in some way concerned with the predicament of human beings living in the age of science and industrialisation: an age in which technology and religious faith have increasingly come into conflict. This is your world and mine and you will find that even if modern plays are *set* in earlier periods of history, they are still inviting judgements from a modern, scientific perspective.

Second, modern plays in some way reflect the remarkable changes in production, theatre design and technology that occurred towards the end of the nineteenth century and have continued ever since. During this period, we have seen the rise of the director, a person whose job it is to have and impose an artistic concept for a production. In previous periods this responsibility lay with the leading actor but the emergence of an entirely new profession has greatly changed the face of the theatre. Directors such as Stanislavsky, Meyerhold, Brecht, Grotowski and Brook have greatly influenced the way in which playwrights have operated. Theatres too have, of course, always been subject to change, but the rapidity of change in the last hundred years or so has been unprecedented: it is a period which has seen the invention of electric light and has now reached a point where through television we can each have our own theatre. Shapes of stages and theatre buildings have been subject to constant experiment so that playwrights are constantly challenged to rethink their craft. Audiences have also been experimented upon; for example, it is only during the period of modern drama that they have sat in a darkened auditorium. So you must remember that any play you are studying was written for a sophisticated yet frequently changing theatre.

Third, you will find that modern plays, as a result of some of the changes I have mentioned, are very varied in form. They include some extremely long plays, such as Shaw's *Man and Superman* (1901), but also many short ones, such as the one-act plays and brief sketches by Pinter and the play *Breath* (1966) by Beckett that only lasts thirty seconds! There are also plays written for performance by an entire community, such as David Edgar's *Entertaining Strangers* (1986), and plays for a single character like David Hare's *Via Dolorosa* (1998) in which the playwright was also the actor. 'One woman' plays such as Eve Ensler's *The Vagina Monologues* (1998) and Dario Fo's and Franca Rame's *Female Parts* (1981) have also proved popular. To some extent the prevalence of short plays reflects tastes and habits: the pace of modern life generally seems to call for shorter plays; but this new timescale and the interest in plays for single performers also stems from the development of many non-commercial and experimental theatres which have small numbers of performers yet greater freedom to try out new ideas. During the modern period there has been more debate about what theatre was for, who it was intended for, who should create it and where and how it should be performed than at any time in our history. There has also been a recognition that the isolated playwright is not the only person who can create plays, so we have seen the emergence of Companies such as Joint Stock, Shared Experience or Tell Tail Hearts with their emphasis on collaborative modes of working. Such plays as David Edgar's massive dramatisation of *Nicholas Nickleby* (1980) or Helen Edmundson's *The Mill on the Floss* (1994) came about by this way of working. A further, more recent, development has been the emergence of a number of outstanding women playwrights and we shall be looking at some of their work at later stages in this book. In 1958 Shelagh Delaney's *A Taste of Honey* and Ann Jellicoe's *The Sport of My Mad Mother* were produced in London and the following year *A Raisin in the Sun* by the first black African-American woman writer, Lorraine Hansberry, was produced in New York. These, however, were lone female voices and, indeed, as recently as 1982 John Russell Brown named only Delaney and Jellicoe as woman writers in his *Short Guide to Modern British Drama*. However, the picture had begun to change: in the 1970s Caryl Churchill and Pam Jems established themselves as important playwrights and they were joined in the 1980s by Louise Page, the overtly lesbian Sarah Daniels, Timberlake Wertenbaker and Michelene Wandor. In the 1990s Sarah Kane, Diane Samuels, Josie Melia and Judy Upton were among the many important contemporary playwrights.

Among modern plays, however, you will find many that conform to what has become something of a traditional structure of three Acts, each containing one or two scenes, a structure often used by Ibsen and his successors. Such plays present a series of episodes of roughly equal length, each with its own climax. Studying a modern play includes discovering how its particular structure works, but you need to avoid any idea that there is a 'right' way for a playwright to construct a play.

▶ What about film and television?

The period I have defined as belonging to 'modern drama' has also seen the development of a form of drama that can be permanently recorded in performance. We cannot ignore film or television in a study of modern drama but there are important differences from published stage plays that mean that a detailed study of film and television is outside the scope of this book. Almost certainly, you will not be required to study a film or television script as part of a conventional drama course, and the additional factors involved in the making of a film or TV drama mean that you would not be able to explore such a script in practical terms unless you had access to a great deal of equipment.

However, there are some very important points to make. The experience of attending the live performance of a stage play is totally different from watching a film or TV drama. Live performance involves interaction between actors and audience and invariably includes an element of risk. Every performance is subtly different from every other performance and playwrights depend on such variation in emphasis and interpretation for their success and for the continued life of their play. On the other hand, once a play is screened, it is fixed.

It follows from these facts that stage playwrights expect and hope for a long 'run' of their play and many 'revivals', whereas the TV dramatist or writer of a screen play can usually only hope for repeat showings of the same version of their work, and these possibly for a very limited time.

Some playwrights, such as David Mamet, Christopher Hampton and Harold Pinter, have been equally successful in writing for the stage and cinema, and the contemporary British playwright Mike Leigh has shown a mastery of stage, television and film writing. Paula MacGee, whose first play *In Nomine Patris* (1983) was concerned with sectarian violence in Scottish football supporters, is now also established as a major film and TV writer. Such writers have allowed their work for one medium to enrich the other but, in the broadest sense, the 'language' of film and TV is different from that of the stage. It may well be that you are only able to see a film or TV version of a play you are studying. If this is the case, you should be mindful of the differences and ensure that any critical analysis you may make is based, initially, on the published stage version with its emphasis on audience response and theatrical space.

What is certainly true and significant is that film and television *techniques* have profoundly influenced the writing of plays in the modern age. This is particularly evident in two ways: first, in the use of such devices as 'flashbacks', very short episodes and a wide variety of locations; and second, in the realisation that there are certain things that film and TV can do much *better* than the live theatre. This second factor has forced playwrights to focus on what makes live theatre distinctive and what it can do better than film. The conventions of film, television and the stage are different and we must turn now to consider the central idea of *conventions* in the theatre.

▶ What are stage conventions?

In my description of the ritual of 'theatre' I suggested that there is an unspoken agreement between the audience and the performers. This agreement actually begins with the playwright and the audience. Every member of an audience unconsciously agrees to make certain assumptions to enable them to derive anything from watching a play. The most basic assumption an audience makes is to agree to imagine that the actors they see on stage represent fictitious or actual historical characters. In a similar way, the audience agrees to imagine that the physical space we call 'the stage' frequently represents somewhere else. This is a stage *convention*, and there are others: for example: the 'aside' – words spoken aloud which are heard by the audience but not supposed to be heard by other characters on the stage; the 'soliloquy' – in which a character is supposedly thinking aloud; direct address to the audience or even the pretence that the audience is not there at all.

These are all conventions through which drama works, and the more you think about them, the more you realise their possibilities. Deciding which conventions to use is a vital part of a playwright's work, as is also a decision as to how to make the audience aware of them. As a student of drama you are well on your way to understanding a play if you can recognise and discuss the conventions that are in operation. This, of course, is another reason why the study of film and television is so different, since they use different conventions.

One of the consequences of the enormous amount of experimentation in the modern theatre has been a renewed interest in the conventions of drama. Directors and playwrights have studied a whole range of historic theatre forms and have discussed the nature and purpose of theatre in order to explore the relationship between performers and audiences. Everything from the Ancient Greek Theatre to recent 'stand-up comedy' has been analysed and debated. This has led to a great deal of writing about the theory and practice of the modern stage, much of which you will find helpful in your study; but it has also led to a very wide variety of conventions being adopted by modern dramatists: and that is where we shall begin our study in the next chapter.

Checklist

Key topics covered in this chapter:

- Definition of modern drama and some of its characteristics
- Approaches to the study of drama
- The term 'playtext'
- The ritual of theatre
- Stage conventions
- The main differences between stage and screen drama

▶ Workshop activities

(You may wish to turn to Chapter 4 at this point.)

1. Devise a very short improvised scene in which a single character enters a mysterious room. The scene may be presented with or without speech and the activity may be done in pairs with the second person directing or as an entire group with a single actor and the remainder as audience. Repeat the scene five times in the following ways: with the audience at one end of the room; with the audience surrounding the actor; with the audience on three sides of the actor; with the actor in the light and the audience in the dark; with the actor's performance recorded on video. Now discuss the differences in the various presentations from the point of view of actor, audience and director.

2. Discuss a very short extract from a modern play you are studying and suggest which of the conventions explored in the previous activity might be the basis for an effective presentation of the extract. Try it out and discuss the results.

2 Getting Started

I am now going to guide you through the process that will enable you to make an initial analysis of any play that you might encounter. There are a number of steps to follow and I suggest that you begin with a fairly relaxed reading of the play. You should aim to read through the play as quickly and comfortably as possible. No modern play is likely to take more than a few hours to read and you should get used to the idea of reading it several times at varying levels. Your *first* reading is almost certainly going to be more like reading a novel; you will probably picture the events taking place in real life rather than on a stage, and your response will be emotional, focused on the characters and their situations, rather than the critical, analytic response which we are finally hoping to achieve. Inevitably, therefore, you will probably find yourself wanting to skim over any lengthy stage directions and giving most attention to what the characters say. However, you cannot entirely ignore stage directions because they give essential information that enable you to make sense of the play and will also provide you with important clues as to the conventions being used by the playwright. I need to mention this because it emphasises the fact that the material contained in a modern playtext is a great deal more than dialogue.

As a result of your first reading you should be able to identify a number of *important features* upon which you will be able to build your critical response. If you do not bear these in mind, your reading will be aimless and probably of little value; more important, these features will help you to make sense of your first contact with the play.

▶ Recognising the conventions

From the moment you begin to read the first page of the playtext you will become aware of the conventions that are operating. This will remind you that the playtext is, as I have said earlier, a blueprint for performance. In order to illustrate the way in which conventions are presented to us I am going to look with you at a particularly interesting example. *The Glass Menagerie* by the great American playwright, Tennessee Williams was first performed in 1945 and is one of the most innovative plays in its use of conventions. In this play, Tom Wingfield, a very sensitive man, looks back on his life in a rather run-down St. Louis tenement with his manipulative mother, Amanda, and his sister Laura, who has a physical disability. Laura seems to live only through her collection of glass animals and when, at Amanda's insistence, Tom invites Jim from the warehouse where he works to meet Laura, the evening proves a disaster. Amanda scolds Tom and he leaves home to join the merchant navy. The stage directions begin with a description of an apartment occupied by the Wingfield family:

> *The Wingfield apartment is in the rear of the building, one of those vast hive-like conglomerations of cellular living units that flower as warty growths in overcrowded urban centres of lower-middle-class population and are symptomatic of the impulse of this largest and fundamentally enslaved section of American society to avoid fluidity and differentiation and to exist and function as one interfused mass of automatism.*
> (Tennessee Williams, *The Glass Menagerie*, Penguin, 1959, p. 233)

This extraordinary statement is followed by a detailed description of the alleys and fire escapes surrounding the apartment. Then, however, the playwright begins to explain his conventions: '*The scene is memory and is therefore non-realistic. Memory takes a lot of poetic licence. The interior therefore is rather dim and poetic.*' Having made this assertion, the playwright then goes on to give more detailed instructions concerning the way the play works. He explains that 'at the rise of the curtain' the audience sees the grim rear wall of the Wingfield tenement but that this gradually disappears during the opening speech to reveal the interior of the ground floor. This transformation is to be achieved by means of a gauze, a device which enables settings to be seen by, or be invisible to, the audience according to the position of the stage lighting. In these stage directions Williams also mentions the footlights and the 'fourth wall' – that is, the missing room wall between the stage and the audience – thus making it clear that he has a 'proscenium stage' in mind – the picture frame stage that does not jut out into the audience. So he has established the initial conventions: (1) What we see on stage is a memory. (2) We can see the interior and exterior of the apartment or both simultaneously. (3) The opening through which we see the action is a 'fourth wall'. Such conventions are fairly common and are very much the product of the introduction of electric stage lighting, although gauzes were in use in conjunction with gas lighting. However, the playwright then goes on to introduce some performance conventions with the introduction of the first character, Tom. The stage directions read: *The narrator is an undisguised convention of the play. He takes whatever licence with dramatic convention*

is convenient to his purposes. Tom, therefore, is established both as a character in the play and as narrator who stands outside the play commenting
on the action. His first entrance involves his entering from 'stage left' stop-
ping in the middle of the stage, lighting a cigarette and speaking directly to
the audience. This first speech includes a series of comments on his function in the play:

> TOM. Yes, I have tricks in my pocket, I have things up my sleeve. But I am
> the opposite of a stage magician. He gives you illusion that has the
> appearance of truth. I give you truth in the pleasant disguise of illusion.
> To begin with, I turn back time.
>
> (Tennessee Williams, *The Glass Menagerie*, Penguin, 1959, p. 234)

Tom then goes on to explain that the play is set in the 1930s and outlines
the social background of the play. He then informs the audience that the
scene in front of them takes place in St. Louis and, as the gauze finally rises
to reveal the family sitting at their meal in silence, Tom joins them at the
table and becomes a character in the play. Here Williams has established a
number of additional conventions: (1) There will be direct address to the
audience. (2) The narrator can set the action in any time he wishes. (3) The
play will work through 'flashback' techniques.

It is unusual to have quite so many conventions spelled out by the playwright at the opening of a play, but we can see here a very good example of
stage conventions in operation. What the playwright is actually saying to us
is simply 'This is how my play works', and this is the first feature we need
to be aware of as we study a play, recognising how it is set up on stage and
what conventions are being employed.

At this point we need to examine some of the different conventions that
are available to the modern playwright. Additionally, what we always need
to bear in mind is the fact that these are influenced by the kind of theatre
that the playwright envisages.

▶ Conventions of language

The most common convention in modern drama is for an audience to listen
while actors on stage simulate everyday conversation. This may be combined
with physical aspects of the staging to create a sense of 'realism', although
the writing of realistic dialogue requires very skilled selection by the playwright. In 'realistic' plays, the actors behave as if the audience was invisible
but, as we have seen with *The Glass Menagerie*, it is possible to break this
convention and have an actor address the audience directly. In that play, the

actor behaves as a narrator and so is a very useful device for explaining the shifts of time and location and for commenting upon the action. The 'Common Man' does this most effectively in Robert Bolt's play *A Man for All Seasons* (1960). The convention of direct address to the audience can be a very powerful factor if it is undertaken by a character in the play who speaks directly to the audience whilst retaining their role in the play; this happens with the character of Michael in Brian Friel's *Dancing at Lughnasa* (1990). One of the most chilling moments in modern drama comes towards the end of T.S. Eliot's *Murder in the Cathedral* (1935) when the knights who have just murdered Thomas Becket suddenly turn and make political speeches to the audience, justifying their actions and then ordering the audience to leave. This level of emotional and intellectual involvement of the audience is also used by Bertolt Brecht. A particularly good example is the closing moments of his play *The Good Person of Setzuan* (1938) when the waterseller poses a moral question for the audience and insists that it is their duty to provide an answer. The convention of David Hare's play *Via Dolorosa* (1998) is that the playwright himself comes on stage and relates a narrative directly to the audience. There are no other actors on stage but a host of 'characters' created by the narrative and their speech is reported. This may seem to defy some of the other conventions of theatre but it is a reminder that 'story telling' is a vital ingredient of all drama and Hare's 'monologue' is only an extension of a device that has been used to great effect by such writers as Harold Pinter and Samuel Beckett.

In plays written in verse everyday talk is not *simulated* but *represented*. The audience agrees to believe that the characters are speaking 'normally' when the language is shaped to include the imagery and power that can be expressed in poetry. Experiments in writing modern verse plays centred around the 1930s and 40s and plays by T.S. Eliot, W.H. Auden and Christopher Fry enjoyed some success. These playwrights argued that verse was able to deal more effectively with the issues they wished to write about; by writing in verse, they claimed that they were rediscovering the essential ritual of theatre. Verse of various kinds is used throughout the modern period: for example, in David Edgar's play *Destiny* (1976) some characters converse in rhyming couplets, whereas in the play *Promenade* (1965) by the versatile Cuban-born playwright Maria Irene Fornes, the entire script consists of poetic utterance. The use of heightened, non-realistic language in some form always remains an option for the dramatist and it need not be conventional verse. The incantation-like dialogue in *Observe the Sons of Ulster Marching Towards the Somme* (1986) creates the effect of nightmarish memories for some of the characters. David Edgar, however, in the play *Teendreams* (1979), which he wrote for the all-women's theatre company Monstrous Regiment, juxtaposes verses from rock songs by Suzi Quatro with the action; whereas Debbie Horsefield in her play about Manchester United football supporters, *Red Devils* (1983), uses the chance of the soccer terraces to enhance her action. In perhaps the most extreme example, Peter Barnes, in his play *The Ruling Class* (1969), gives one of his characters, the Earl of Gurney, several speeches in complete gibberish to simulate an elderly Peer addressing the House of Lords.

Audiences make another kind of imaginative leap with the language conventions of Brian Friel's *Translations* (1980). In this play about the English 'redcoat' soldiers in Ireland, we are asked to believe that some of the characters are speaking in English and others in Gaelic. In fact, all the dialogue is in English, but the audience has to assume that the characters supposedly speaking Gaelic cannot be understood by the English soldiers.

I do not want to give the impression that a playwright selects only one convention and uses that throughout a play. *The Glass Menagerie* shows us a good number of conventions operating at the same time. When it comes to language, a playwright may vary the conventions, moving for example from dialogue to monologue. In John Godber's play *Bouncers* (1977) we see some realistic re-enactments of the experiences of four bouncers working in a nightclub, but their actions are punctuated by monologues that the characters direct straight to the audience. In these monologues the bouncers reveal their inner feelings in a way that contrasts sharply with their communal behaviour. In a rather similar fashion Sean O'Casey moves from realistic prose to verse in his play *The Silver Tassie* (1928). Whereas the more domestic scenes are spoken in everyday conversational language, O'Casey relies on poetic prose and verse to evoke the horror of life in the trenches of the First World War.

The language convention of a play may depend upon its sources. For example A.R. Gurney's play *Love Letters* (1984) consists entirely of a playtext derived from the letters written by two lovers. The play is staged with the two characters sitting on opposite sides of the stage and the drama emanates from the reading and writing of letters between the two of them. We accept the convention that a character may be writing a letter but reading it aloud at the same time or that a character receiving a letter will also read it aloud. Thus an inner drama becomes externalised through the convention of performance. Another play based on letters was James Roose-Evans's *84 Charing Cross Road* (1985), which he adapted for the stage from a book by Helene Hanff of the same name. In this play an entire relationship begins with the writing and receiving of letters. Other 'documentary' sources such as diaries, newspaper reports, or legal papers have increasingly been incorporated into the playtexts of modern plays, and their performance very often involves the convention in which the physical action is frozen while a character speaks the words of the document in a 'neutral' voice. A very good example of the extensive use of documentary sources is Barrie Keeffe's play *Better Times* (1985), which charts the events of the famous Poplar riots in 1919.

▶ The play-within-the-play

Most plays in the realistic tradition tend not to draw attention to the fact that they are being performed in a theatre. The convention is that the audience believes that what they witness is a re-enactment of reality and that, in some sense, they really *are* present as invisible spectators. As we have seen in *The Glass Menagerie*, this convention can be effectively broken so that the audience is reminded that the events taking place are, in fact, simply a theatrical happening.

There are, however, some plays in which the whole nature of theatre is exploited, explored and celebrated. In such plays, the process of creating drama is itself the subject. This is certainly the case in a play by Peter Weiss which has what must be the clumsiest title in modern drama: *The Persecution and Murder of Marat as Performed by the Inmates of the Asylum of Charenton under the Direction of the Marquis de la Sade* (1964) which was originally produced in Germany. This play, usually known as *The Marat/Sade*, was first directed in Britain by the great English director Peter Brook and he created a most disturbing experience for the audience. Brook's production not only created the impression that the audience was physically in the asylum but also provided them with the uncomfortable sensation of having their applause mocked by the performers. Thus the drama worked on a variety of levels: the inmates were themselves deeply disturbed individuals and their behaviour revealed this; but involving them in creating a play performance within the broader structure of the whole play showed another level of disturbed behaviour. Not surprisingly, of course, the drama enabled some of the characters to find new identities in the roles that they played in the re-enactment of the murder of Marat.

Another group of potentially difficult individuals performing a play was the subject of Timberlake Wertenbaker's *Our Country's Good* (1988). In this play, a group of convicts arrives in Australia in 1788 and it is decided by the officers guarding them that they will act a play. The play chosen is the eighteenth-century comedy, *The Recruiting Officer*, and we watch the progress of the play through the early castings and rehearsal right to its final performance. The convention is that the audience is both the audience for *Our Country's Good* and eventually for *The Recruiting Officer*, but there is also an 'on-stage' audience for the latter. Wertenbaker's play actually concludes with the performance of *The Recruiting Officer* just about to begin.

Interestingly enough, *Our Country's Good* was given a very moving production in a British prison in the presence of Timberlake Wertenbaker in 1990, where the audience clearly found themselves associating with the action in unexpected ways. In Alan Ayckbourn's dark comedy *Season's Greetings* (1980), an inept uncle insists on mounting his annual puppet play during family festivities and the bizarre events of the puppet play throw the domestic drama into comic relief.

The plays I have just described not only celebrate theatrical conventions but they also play with them and you should be aware of these techniques as you make your first reading of a text. The less a play draws attention to itself as a play, the more 'realistic' it is likely to seem. Conversely, the more it focuses on itself as a play, the more questions it may be raising about how we perceive certain issues.

▶ Conventions of time

Every play performance takes place in 'real time', but through the conventions of drama it can inhabit imaginary time. The stage directions of a play may simply read *'Time: the present'*, but you will recall that in *The Glass Menagerie* the narrator, Tom, says 'I turn back time'. In this particular play the events take place in the 1930s and this is clearly stated by the narrator; however, other playwrights have less direct ways of informing their audiences that their play is set in the past. Conventions may include the wearing of 'period' costumes or speaking in a way that we would identify with an earlier time. Plays may, of course, be set in the future and in these cases, as with David Campton's *Lunatic View* (1956), the content has to be entirely imaginary. Through conventions the playwright establishes the time at which the events are taking place.

Plays also are able to span periods of time. Some hours or even years may separate the events of successive scenes and again the playwright has to find a convention by which this information can be conveyed. In Brecht's play *Mother Courage and her Children* (1938) the events portrayed extend from the spring of 1624 to January 1636. This information is given to the audience through a series of statements or projections at the beginning of each scene. There are, in fact, a good number of plays in the tradition of what is known as 'epic theatre' in which this technique is used. Other conventions may have to indicate the passage of time through the fading of light or the behaviour of the characters.

Time has been of particular interest to modern dramatists. J.B. Priestley, for example, experimented in several of his plays with aspects of time. *Time and the Conways* (1937) works through a convention in which events are seen in reverse sequence. The opening scene shows the most recent events, and the final scene, the most distant. Harold Pinter has used precisely the same convention in his play *Betrayal* (1980). But Priestley was not satisfied with so simple an experiment. In *An Inspector Calls* (1946) the play ends with an event that closely resembles the play's opening and we begin to wonder if, in some sense, time is cyclic. Priestley adds to this unusual treatment of time by having the same setting for each part of the play viewed from a different angle.

A very good example of the importance of recognising and understanding the conventions being used by a dramatist comes in Charlotte Keatley's play *My Mother said I never should* (1988). This play concerns the lives of four women born as far apart as 1900 and 1971. However, at times in the play, the four women meet as children and in these scenes they wear clothes contemporary to their own generation. Obviously these meetings are a fantasy but they are 'real' for the sense of the play. The rest of the action consists of scenes involving the various women at different times in their lives. For example, there is a scene in 1987 in which the characters are listening to 'walkmans', whereas there is another in 1979 in which one of the characters is carrying her favourite doll. These short scenes do not necessarily take place in sequence of time and so, in a sense, some of them are flashbacks. The total effect of the play enables the audience to see the complex issues affecting the lives of the four women and is very much based on the techniques of film and television. Similar techniques are employed by Mary Morris in *Too Far to Walk* (2002), a play that spans over sixty years and explores the lives of two very different sisters. Any description or analysis of such plays that ignored the conventions would be of very little value.

▶ Conventions of space

In the play I have just described, Charlotte Keatley says in her opening stage directions: 'The setting should simply be a magic place where things can happen.' This sense that a stage is a space that can be transformed into any location that the playwright wishes is a part of a major convention of theatre. It has been explored in a very influential way in Peter Brook's *The Empty Space* (1965), a manifesto that every student of modern drama will encounter at some time. Playwrights determine the way in which space is used. For example, in the play *Fanshen* (1976) by David Hare, an empty stage space is used to represent many locations within a Chinese village. The opening scene shows peasants working the land and yet the same space becomes a venue for meetings and discussion. Multiple settings for the action, then, can be represented by a single space.

We have seen that in *The Glass Menagerie* the playwright clearly has a particular kind of staging in mind. He uses the convention of the proscenium stage with gauzes, footlights and a curtain that rises and falls. Other modern playwrights have used very different forms of staging as the basis of their drama. One of the most daring of contemporary British playwrights, Alan Ayckbourn, derives many of his ideas from the fact that he works regularly in a Theatre in the Round. His plays include situations where the audience views several levels of a house simultaneously even though the actors themselves are left to convey this information by pretending to mount stairs. He has also experimented with plays in which the audience watches the action in two bedrooms at virtually the same time.

Perhaps, however, the single most powerful convention relating to stage space is the audience's agreement to imagine that the doors and other entrances and exits on a stage lead to another part of the same imaginary world. This 'off-stage' life is shown in a play like Arthur Miller's *The Crucible* (1953) in which we become aware of the court proceedings in an adjacent room. Once again, Ayckbourn is the boldest of experimental practitioners: in his trio of plays *The Norman Conquests* (1974) the action in each play consists of what happens off-stage in another of the plays. It requires attendance on three consecutive nights to see the entire action. Our belief that beyond the doors in a stage set there lies something other than the wing space of the theatre is vital if we are to enter into the intensity of the dramas unfolding. Ibsen's *A Doll's House* (1879) ends with the main female character leaving the house and slamming the door. This pivotal moment in the development of modern drama could hardly have worked without the acceptance of the convention of off-stage life.

The period that we describe as 'modern drama' shows wide experimentation in the use of stage space as well as conventions of language and time and this has led to a wide variety of techniques that dramatists can employ, sometimes mixing them in the same play in order to produce further dramatic effects.

Checklist

Key topics covered in this chapter:

- What is meant by a convention
- Examples of many kinds of stage conventions
- Examples of plays using various conventions
- The importance of recognising stage conventions

▶ Workshop activities

1. Select a number of newspaper articles and devise a scene based on their contents. Find ways of staging your scene using a number of the conventions mentioned in this chapter.
2. Write an imaginary letter that can then be presented as a series of flashbacks.
3. Gather together a number of modern playtexts and examine the stage directions for the opening scenes. Compare the different techniques being used and discuss the possibility of alternative conventions for each play.
4. Arrange an acting area in which a scene is to take place. Devise a scene in which two characters meet and experiment with various conventions as follows: direct address to the audience, monologue and dialogue, multiple locations and off-stage life.

3 What Can I Achieve in a First Reading?

By now you should be familiar with the idea of conventions and be able to recognise any that you encounter fairly easily. Now we need to turn to the other general aspects of a play that you ought to be able to deal with in a first reading. As an example I want you to imagine that you are required to study Arthur Miller's play *Death of a Salesman*, written in 1948. You may know nothing about the playwright except, perhaps, that he was once married to Marilyn Monroe and that in terms of dates he fits the label 'modern dramatist'.

▶ Action

The second general aspect of the play that you should be able to discuss after an initial reading is what actually *happens*. Be careful here, though. Students often place far too much emphasis on this element and so offer a summary of the story-line or plot instead of a critical commentary. One reason for this is that they fail to distinguish between the play's *story*, its *action* and its *performance*. A play tells a story and the outline of that story must be clear in your mind by the time you finish your first reading of the play. So, for example, we can say that Miller's *Death of a Salesman* tells the story of a salesman named Willy Loman and how his life slowly disintegrates into failure until he finally kills himself.

This story, however, is not told in a straightforward chronological sequence; and here the conventions of time come into prominence. Instead, events from the past are interspersed among scenes from the present. Strictly speaking, the story actually begins in the scenes set furthest in the past, but the action of the play begins in the present. What the *action* of the play does is to show and explain the death of Willy Loman by a deliberate juxtaposing of scenes and effects. As you read a play, you should be aware of this distinction between story and action: think of the action of the play as *the way* in which the story is presented and organised so as to bring out its meaning. *Death of a Salesman*, for example, clearly tells the story of Loman's life and death;

the action of the play, however, shows us how he is a victim of the American Dream of modern society and of its values.

One complication that you need to be aware of is that the action of a play embraces *all* that occurs during a *performance* of a play. Such a performance is obviously impossible to reproduce just by reading, but what you can seize upon to help you grasp the full action of the play is the *activity* in a theatrical performance. The actors playing the characters in *Death of a Salesman* are given dozens of activities by the playwright. They drink, get out of bed, move in specified ways, smoke, laugh, and so on. Modern plays are, in fact, dense with such instructions and clearly you cannot hope to retain all these details even after several readings. This does not make them unimportant; on the contrary; playwrights since Ibsen have found it essential to provide minute details of the activities of their characters so as to convey a full sense of them as human beings caught in a particular world, and we can never hope to grasp the meaning of a play without considering these issues. However, this is a matter for detailed scene study or workshop experience rather than general reading, and it is quite sufficient if, on your first contact with the play, you allow these activities to give your reading imaginative life. If you can remember one or two details of such activities – for example, in *Death of a Salesman* we constantly see characters going to the refrigerator, or sitting alone at the family table – that would be a bonus, for it will help you discipline your thinking by having something concrete to build on.

▶ The protagonist's predicament

Our next consideration is the predicament of the central character or *protagonist.* Plays inevitably show characters in struggle against some problem or series of problems that threaten to overwhelm them. In modern drama the *protagonist* or *hero* usually possesses so few of the heroic qualities traditionally associated with that title that we often use the expression *antihero,* while the problems confronted by this character are domestic rather than on the grand, cosmic scale of characters such as Shakespeare's Hamlet. At a personal level, however, the outcome may be equally tragic, disturbing or harrowing.

By the conclusion of your first reading of the play you should be able to summarise both the action of the play and the predicament of the protagonist. The effect on you as a reader will be cumulative, because as you progress through the play further complications of the predicament will arise. It is a good idea to make a note of them as you go.

Willy Loman's main predicament is that he is in a situation for which he is entirely unfitted: he must live and support his family from his earnings as a salesman, yet his personality militates against his being a success; he lives in an enclosed space, yet his nature longs for wide open spaces. He has also added to his predicament by making a number of fatal errors of judgement: his brief unfaithfulness to his wife Linda has permanently poisoned his relationship with his favourite son and the attitudes he has encouraged in Biff have contributed to the latter's failure in 'math' at school. Willy has manufactured a network of lies in which he has become trapped, so that he is trapped in three ways: by his job, by his house and environment and by his own deceit. Ultimately, there is only one means of escape – his death by suicide.

As we look at the conventions of the play we see that Arthur Miller has chosen particularly effective means by which to establish Willy Loman's predicament, and the résumé I have offered only suggests the level of awareness you might reasonably be expected to achieve after a single, fairly rapid reading. The issues are by no means exhausted, but if you pay close attention to both the action and the predicament of the main character, you should be able to say in general terms what the play you are studying is about.

▶ Tensions and threats

Much of the fascination of plays stems from the interaction between the different characters in the same way that this is often what makes real life interesting. This aspect of a play only emerges fully in performance, but even at the early reading stage it is possible and, indeed, essential, to identify the sources of tension. The protagonist's predicament often engulfs and is frequently derived from other characters, yet we must not neglect to notice the tensions between lesser characters as well. *Identifying the sources of tension* between characters is another function of your first reading and, again, it is something you should note down as you read.

An interest in the way that people relate to each other is a particular feature of modern drama, just as in modern communication studies there is an interest in what is called 'inter-personal' communications. This is all partly a result of the developing science of psychology that was in its infancy when Ibsen wrote his first naturalistic play in the late nineteenth century. Modern playwrights are operating in a world that generally attempts to explain people's behaviour in rational, scientific terms and that sees individuals as needing to succeed in their personal relationships in order to achieve a sense of well-being and social adjustment. Social order and personal happiness are threatened by tensions between individuals or groups; tensions force us into playing different roles, adapting our behaviour to suit a situation, while tensions themselves may also become obsessive fears.

If there were no tensions in a play or in life itself there would be perfect harmony but little interest. In drama, as in life, we look for a resolution of tensions and that is what makes characters in plays struggle on. The tramps in Beckett's *Waiting for Godot* (1953), for example, endure a restless state of waiting because there is hope that when Godot comes there will be some kind of resolution. Davies, the old tramp in Harold Pinter's *The Caretaker* (1960), struggles to find a way of resolving the tension that has developed between himself and his new landlord, Aston.

The major sources of tension in a play should therefore be one of your first concerns. The first few pages of *Death of a Salesman* show how relatively easy the tensions are to spot. As Willy replies to Linda's first questions about his day, there is already a hint of irritation and of reluctance to give a straight answer. When Willy does explain his utter exhaustion, Linda's reply contains an element of refusal to face the facts. Soon we learn of tension between Willy and his employers, a frightening tension between Willy and his son Biff, and also of conflicting perceptions of each other by father and son. Characters and situations also pose *threats* to other characters. For example, we feel that Willy Loman sees Charley, his neighbour, as a threat to his self-esteem; Bernard, one of Biff's contemporaries and rivals, threatens to expose the false values that Willy has instilled into his son; and, above all, the *past* threatens every aspect of Willy's present life. The past means that Willy must always delude himself and others, and this creates constant tension.

In your critical response to a play you are going to have to evaluate the dramatist's method of showing the tensions and threats that govern the behaviour of the characters that have been created. During and *just after* your first reading you will be concentrating on what characters say and do in the context of their developing situations, and you should ensure that you have a clear idea of the main features of the relationships between the characters. You may need to go back over the play very quickly to check details and impressions and you may find it helpful to draw a diagram consisting of circles representing each character and arrows joining them indicating possible causes of tension. You may have to ask such questions as 'Does she suspect him?' or 'Did one event in the past affect this relationship?' So many modern plays examine the effect of the past on the present that this second question is almost inevitable.

▶ Identifying the world of the play and its social order

In addition to having some clear ideas about the kinds of tension that exist in the play you are studying, you should come from your first reading with a clear sense of the kind of world that the play is about. For the purposes of a play the writer creates an entire fictional world in which to set the action, even if that world is based on historical fact. That world may be totally unfamiliar to us, as in Arthur Miller's *The Crucible*, or remarkably familiar to us, as in *Death of a Salesman*. In either case, as readers and audience, we must believe in its reality and grasp its characteristics and pressures. Understanding the world of the play may require some research on your part but it is usually possible to form a fairly clear impression of it on your first reading.

The world of *Death of a Salesman* is modern consumer society: a world in which people buy goods with built-in obsolescence on credit and struggle to pay off mortgages for the rest of their lives. Technology produces new gadgets that the wealthy use for pleasure and the not-so-wealthy feel pressurised into buying. The other half of that world consists of the salespeople themselves, dedicated to enticing people to spend, sometimes having to drive thousands of miles, with their success depending on the precarious business of getting people to part with their money. The gap between success and failure in the world of sales is perilously narrow. Salespeople must cultivate 'push', 'drive' and ruthlessness. This is a society that treats its individuals like its goods – they can be thrown away once they are worn out – but during their useful lives they can be kept in boxes. The pressures on individuals and families caught up in such a situation are immense and inevitably parents hope for better things for their children.

If we are entirely honest, nothing about the world of *Death of a Salesman* should come as a surprise: even if much of the sales pressure is now exerted by telephone, we know that our world is full of advertisements for salespeople who will recklessly drive their cars and themselves in the hope of rich rewards, but the promise of high earnings for the successful are frequently phoney. We continue to house our population in cramped conditions which exclude the possibility of a garden or even of sunlight; true, the latest electrical 'necessity' may no longer be the tape recorder, as it is in the play, but its contemporary equivalent is all too obvious. So, in some respects, the fact that *Death of a Salesman* is set in the late 1940s is almost irrelevant provided we understand the *kind* of world the play establishes.

All that I have discussed so far can easily be derived from a first reading of the play, but it is also important that you link it to the broader *social order* presented and subsequently threatened by the events of the play. Human beings attempt to live in a society by creating the sense of social order, and in a play it is quite easy to identify this ideal state towards which a particular society is striving. In *Death of a Salesman*, for example, it is clear that the family is seen as the basis of society, and also as an ideal of social concern. From the very opening of the play tenderness and concern are expressed by a wife for her husband; the father feels love and anxiety for his sons; home is the base to which they all come and in which the mother has a central, caring role. The disappointment in Biff that Willy endures seems to be a product of a father's legitimate pride and aspirations; the pressure on Willy partially stems from his having to provide for his family. It is all the more important for us to grasp that this sense of order is threatened because it is based on illusions and delusions.

Think, now, of the wider social order of adulthood and work shown in this play. Willy's sons, Happy and Biff, 'ought to be' married, with families and careers of their own. Having a career is supposed to provide challenge and fulfilment; workers should be respected, while long and valued service to a company ought to be recognised; a man should be able to own a house, a car and a refrigerator without a constant sense of burden. In personal relations there should be sensitivity, gratitude and an appreciation of personal dignity.

These are the features of the social order that the characters in *Death of a Salesman* are trying to build. It is painfully obvious from a very early stage that it will crumble, and part of the fascination of the first reading is to see how and to what extent it does. You should always try to summarise briefly the world of the play you are studying and the particular features of the social order that underpin all the play's action. *The Glass Menagerie* provides a very similar picture to *Death of a Salesman* because it is also based on the American Dream, but some plays may provide a much narrower or wider perspective. Beckett's *Waiting for Godot*, for example, concentrates entirely upon two tramps who remain by a roadside throughout the entire play and who have established their own social order that hardly relates to the rest of the world. Their social order is threatened by the two appearances of Lucky and Pozzo and the non-appearance of a mysterious Mr Godot. In contrast, again, Miller's *The Crucible* presents a complex society structured around the authority of families and employers in relation to the ultimate authority of the Bible and the Church.

A few sentences describing your understanding of these essential features of a play will provide you with an overall grasp of the larger significance of the play you are studying and it will show you how it is about much broader issues than the experiences of particular characters. You should be able to demonstrate how the play deals with the larger questions of the place of human beings within the social order.

▶ Conducting your initial analysis: a step-by-step guide, with example

By this stage you may be feeling somewhat overwhelmed by all that you are expected to achieve in a single reading. There is no need to panic: we all have our own comfortable rate of absorption, and if it takes you two or more readings to complete what is set out here to your satisfaction, then that is perfectly reasonable. The important point to grasp, however, is that whatever line your study of a play will eventually take or whatever question you are trying to answer, there is no point in going on to more specific or detailed study until you have mastered the material by using the steps suggested here:

- Recognise the conventions
- Achieve a broad outline of the action
- Define the protagonist's predicament
- Trace the main tensions and threats
- Examine the world of the play and its social order

In order to illustrate how these basic steps can be used to approach a modern play, and how to draw things together, it might be helpful if we work through a further brief example before we move on to the next stage. The play I have chosen to concentrate on here is *The Caretaker* (1960) by Harold Pinter and I shall be making some comparisons as we go along with both *Death of a Salesman* and *The Glass Menagerie*.

1. Recognise the conventions
The process of recognising the conventions of a play is often a simple matter of observation. At the opening of *The Caretaker* the stage directions give a very explicit description of a room, including precise positioning of the furniture, and equally detailed instructions for the behaviour of the characters. There is no mention of a narrator or of any very obvious theatrical device and we can assume that the basic conventions are 'realistic'.

The play is divided into three acts: Act II takes place only a few seconds after Act I, but there is a lapse of two weeks between Acts II and III. Within the acts there are recognisable 'scenes' and the playwright frequently uses lighting to evoke the passage of time, making particularly effective use of 'blackouts'. There are no flashbacks and the events take place in sequence. Characters speak in conversational language, including pauses and periods of silence, and at one point there is a very extended monologue in which a character speaks in the beam of a single spotlight. However, there is no attempt at direct address to the audience. It all seems, then, very straightforward if rather bare and ordinary.

Once we have considered the other important features of the play we can return to these conventions and make more sense of them.

2. Achieve a broad outline of the action
In certain respects not a great deal actually 'happens' in *The Caretaker*; although the playwright has provided a great deal of *activity* for the actors,

there are relatively few major incidents. Much of the play's action is taken up with talk in which the characters generally fail to communicate with each other. This failure is a key to the real action of the play, which remains taut and compelling throughout. At some points characters even use language to intimidate each other.

The action of the play is set in a single junk-filled room and occupies four days plus a further two days a fortnight later. After a mysterious opening in which a man, who turns out to be Mick, sits on a bed looking up at a bucket into which water is dripping and then leaves the stage, Aston (Mick's brother) brings in Davies, a tramp who he has rescued from a brawl in a café. The shy Aston treats Davies kindly and asks him if he would like to be caretaker. Davies, who shows himself to be entirely self-regarding and who brags pathetically, grudgingly accepts. Davies's past and even his identity are doubtful but Aston continues to treat him with kindness and reveals a great deal about himself in a long monologue. Meanwhile, Mick has been observing Davies and alternately scares him and leads him on with the offer of the job of caretaker. Davies, foolishly thinking that he has gained Mick's confidence, becomes openly aggressive towards Aston and eventually threatens and taunts him with references to mental illness. Aston, with an immense effort, suggests that Davies should leave and when Davies turns to Mick for support he finds himself abruptly dismissed from his 'caretaking'. Desperately, Davies now turns back to Aston, suggesting that he take over Aston's bed; but this is a final encroachment and the play ends with Aston turning away.

If you have read or seen *The Caretaker* you will know that this summary of the play's action does not give any hint of some of its more disturbing activities, such as the incident when Aston and Mick throw Davies's bag around the stage in a bizarre teasing game reminiscent of the fooling around of Laurel and Hardy. You will often notice such puzzling things in modern plays, but don't let this deter you from achieving a clear sense of the play's overall action; don't allow the details of the play to prevent you from getting hold of its basic action.

3. Define the protagonist's predicament

The first tricky question is 'Who *is* the protagonist?' In terms of interest and the number of lines they speak, the characters of Aston and Davies seem about equal. Is this, then, a play like *Waiting for Godot*, where there are clearly *two* protagonists? You may wish to argue differently, but the fact that every scene shows one or both of the brothers relating to the tramp Davies, who is on stage for all but the opening minute of the play, suggest that Davies is the central character. Pinter reinforces this by naming the play *The Care-taker*, the role that Davies is supposed to fill.

Davies, the protagonist, is used to sleeping rough; he is defensive, absurdly prejudiced and racist, vague about the past, and apparently threatened by almost everybody with whom he comes into contact. He is a social outcast with no roots, no hope, no social confidence and no realistic ambitions. His world is governed by where he will scrounge his next cup of tea or pair of shoes. Suddenly he is offered the chance of a permanent base, but he cannot understand the environment into which he has been brought, nor the two people who inhabit or visit it. Desperately he has to try to readjust to their conduct and at the same time to contend with his own contradictory ragbag of attitudes. The longer he stays, the more comfortable he becomes in the physical sense, but the more futile are his efforts to break into the tight framework that exists before he came. Clearly, he cannot respond adequately to the demands of this situation.

4. Trace the main tensions and threats in the play

Although there are only three characters in this play, there are certain points where there is tension between all of them. Such tension is suggested at the very beginning when Mick leaves the stage *before* Aston enters with Davies. There is clearly a strange relationship between the two brothers. Davies seems uncomfortable but is gradually relaxed by Aston's kind behaviour. However, Davies then questions the nature of the room – who is outside, who shares the bathroom, why is there a broken window, the junk, the gas stove. Such criticism seems unacceptable to Aston; it even seems ungrateful. Davies's snorings and gibberings in the night and, later, his smell upset Aston and deprive him of sleep. The tramp's response is aggressive and he views Aston with increasing incomprehension.

Mick manipulates tension by leaving Davies wriggling like a fish on a hook. There is a famous scene where Davies's bag and trousers are passed back and forth and Aston has to intervene to break the pattern. Twice Mick terrifies and intimidates Davies and the tramp lives in the continual aftermath of these incidents. When, however, Davies thinks he has detected a way of undermining Aston by exploiting any possible gulf between the brothers, Mick closes the gap, violently. We suspect that, in a strange way, Mick may be afraid of his brother Aston.

All the characters in *The Caretaker* feel threatened: Aston by the world outside and by the intrusion of Davies when he seeks to upset the social order; Davies, by authority, bureaucracy, the past, questions and by anything or anybody he doesn't understand; Mick, by Aston's introduction of Davies. Mick uses violence and language to threaten Davies; an obscure sense of menace from the outside broods over the entire play.

5. Examine the world of the play and its social order

The Caretaker deals with people who live in the run-down, seedy environment of a present-day city suburb. Large houses that were once considered rather 'smart' are now divided into flats, and people of various races and at the bottom of the income-scale live in the dingy accommodation provided. It is an area of small cafés, junk shops and pubs; there is little sense of community in the broad meaning of that word; there is suspicion and prejudice between racial groups. We would probably describe the environment as being one of 'social deprivation' and yet this is a world in which a small minority *own* property and make decisions that affect the lives of others. It is a fundamentally materialistic society and there are some who drop out of the 'rat race' and become regarded as 'odd'. A particularly potent example of this is the treatment of mental illness, that has become impersonal and even brutal, no adequate provision being made for the reintegration of patients into society. In a similar way, *The Glass Menagerie* shows us a society in which attitudes to physical disability are equally unenlightened.

Mick has been relatively successful: he is a quick thinker and smooth talker, so he feels at ease in the world. He has acquired a property in a state of some dilapidation and has allowed his brother, Aston, to live in part of it. By contrast, Aston is mild and incompetent, slow to make decisions and unable to act upon them. He makes few demands on life and lives surrounded by various objects he has accumulated, obviously finding some security in them. He dreams only of the shed he will one day build in the garden although there seems to be no prospect that he will do so. The arrangement between Mick, who is obviously concerned for his brother, and Aston, who is a 'drop out', clearly suits them both. Although to outside eyes the room in which Aston lives, cluttered with useless junk, seems absurd, to him it represents familiarity, security and a place of refuge. When a new character, Davies, is introduced into the room, the whole social order is threatened.

You may feel that you could not sum up your impressions of the play you are studying in the way that I have after just a single reading. My advice is for you to take your time and establish a firm grasp of the five features I have described. What will help you to do this is if you can see how *The Caretaker* and *Death of a Salesman* are built around a common pattern, a common tension between, on the one hand, the idea of social order, and, on the other, the idea of disorder, threats and tensions that undermine that order. If you keep this pattern in mind it will help you clarify all the five features I have described, as it will also help you move forward in your study of the play as a play: something seen and acted. In other words, you will start to come to grips with the play as a piece of drama rather than as a story with speaking characters.

If you are fortunate enough to begin your study of a play by seeing it performed in a theatre you should be able to make use of the steps I have described as a means of making sense of the experience. The impact of a live performance is obviously different from a reading, because in the theatre you are responding to a succession of images carefully shaped by the playwright, director and actors. Your reading *must* take account of what happens in performance if you are to do full justice to the play, and in order to do this you need to return to reconsider the conventions. We can now make this into another step: *think about the play in performance.*

6. Think about the play in performance

We can briefly summarise the main conventions for this purpose as being: language; setting; plot, action and activity.

(1) Studying a play involves an examination of the style, form and content of the language, and at this stage you should notice its general characteristics. Notice, for example, which characters do the most speaking; note any particularly long speeches and to whom characters are speaking. As we have seen, some modern playwrights give their speeches directly addressed to the audience; other characters appear to speak mainly to themselves while other plays give the impression of normal conversation.

Both *The Caretaker* and *Death of a Salesman* provide excellent examples of the way in which language works through the conventions of performance. Aston's huge speech that concludes Act II of Pinter's play is probably the longest speech you will encounter in any play and seems rather unacceptable on the page. Quite apart from its rather slow and tedious progress, it seems incredible that anyone would really talk for that long. Yet, in the theatre, this speech, delivered in the narrowing circle of a single spotlight with the baffled Davies looking on, is a gripping experience, invariably felt in intense silence by the audience.

In *Death of a Salesman* we accept without difficulty that Happy and Biff are talking in their bedroom but that we can also hear Willy's words from the living room. At times we also receive a particular impression from the juxtaposition of the words of the play with the sound of a flute. In the same way, a play may include moments when we, the audience, hear what a character on stage is saying whilst the other characters on stage do not. The opening of *The Caretaker* is made especially effective through the use of yet another language convention: 'voices off'.

(2) Many modern plays, such as *The Caretaker*, are set in a single room and you should reflect back on what I have said about realistic settings and the idea of a 'fourth wall'. In this play, it is the junk cluttering Aston's room

that is so important. The whole meaning of the play depends on seeing Aston in this environment. Objects such as the bucket hanging from the ceiling, the gas stove, the window or the Buddha are as much a part of the play as the language or the characters with which students tend to become preoccupied. *Death of a Salesman* works through the convention of the multiple setting. Here the playwright enables us to witness several rooms in a house simultaneously and we can see how powerful a convention this is when we imagine how revealing it would be to be able to do this in real life! The same flexibility enables Arthur Miller to move backwards and forwards in time, a feature with which Pinter himself has experimented in more recent plays.

Perhaps the most significant demand Miller makes at the beginning of *Death of a Salesman* is in the stage directions: *We are aware of towering, angular shapes behind it, surrounding it on all sides.* This might remind you of similarly evocative descriptions at the opening of *The Glass Menagerie*. When you read such directions on the first page of a play, it is very easy to forget them by the second page, but it is the playwright's intention that we should never forget them; in the theatre we are never allowed to.

(3) Telling a story in the theatre, which is what all plays actually do, is very different from telling it in a novel or narrative poem. The playwright selects events to be shown in a given time and may decide that these events are causally linked or simply acquire significance by being seen in a certain sequence.

Death of a Salesman begins with Willy's arriving home. It is not the only time he has arrived home like this, and yet, in another sense, there has never been a moment like this. *The Caretaker*, by contrast, begins with Mick sitting on a bed looking at a bucket suspended from a ceiling. Very cleverly, though, Pinter thwarts our expectations by having Mick exit before he has spoken and before we can discover anything about him. Neither playwright has made an arbitrary decision about the starting moment and there is no reason at all why a play should not begin a few seconds before someone gets up and leaves the room. When we study a play, however, we do need to examine the impact of the moment when 'the curtain rises'.

Once the action has begun, the plot unfolds. Quite possibly, the juxtaposition of events, the coincidences, the carefully contrived suspense and climaxes combine to create a highly improbable story. But this rarely strikes us in performance; it is more likely to have already struck you in reading. The greatest single problem in reading a play, however, is to envisage the action; for example, it is so easy to forget the existence of a character if he or she remains silent for a long time. Think of the silent figure of Davies watching and listening to Aston's tremendous speech about his illness. In a performance, characters are moving all the time, or if they remain still their very stillness makes a visual statement. Linda's mending of the lining of Willy's jacket or Aston's fiddling with the plug on a toaster are not extraneous details: they arise from the very essence of the story and you must recognise them as something to be investigated as part of a critical response.

7. Draw your initial analysis together

You will now have read the entire play enough times to satisfy yourself that you could answer questions about it in a way that shows you have thought about it in broad terms and can imagine it being performed in a theatre. You will now be able to draw upon this understanding for a much closer look at the text. Before you go on to do that, it is a good idea to stand back from the play you are studying and try to draw your thoughts together by asking yourself some simple questions:

- Can I now see the play as a piece of action performed on a stage?
- Can I see how conventions are used?
- Can I see how it deals with tensions and threats to the idea of social order?

In other words, just run through the topics your first reading should have covered. Sometimes, you might find it helpful to discover if the playwright has said anything about the intended effect of their play on stage. Miller has provided introductions in the published editions of many of his plays whereas Pinter tends to insist that the meaning of his plays emerges only in performance. Modern theatre criticism also suggests that many of those meanings are 'constructed' by the audience, but that is a topic for later in this book.

A more detailed study of the text will reveal many fascinating layers of meaning and we can conduct this investigation through both practical work and further reading: the topics of my next two chapters.

Checklist

Key topics covered in this chapter:

- Seven steps for studying a play
- An initial analysis using the steps
- Imagining a play in performance from a printed text
- Recognising stage conventions at work
- Some simple questions about your initial reading

▶ Workshop activities

1. Improvise a short event in which Aston, Mick and Davies make a speech in which they say what they are really thinking about each other, OR interview each of them in turn and press them for details of their lives.
2. Devise an improvisation dealing with the American ideal of free enterprise and the pressure to sell yourself to the company.
3. Imagine a conversation between a parent and son or daughter who have totally different concepts of success and yet remain devoted to each other.
4. Act out all the activity in the scene from *The Caretaker* at the end of Act I in which Davies is exploring the contents of the room. What is the effect of all this activity?

4 Practical Workshops for Drama Study

Throughout this book I am suggesting various practical activities to enrich and extend your approach to the study of modern drama. A drama 'workshop' is rather like a laboratory in which experiments are carried out and ideas tested. Indeed, our recent approach through this method owes a great deal both to the Polish director Grotowski who named his theatre a 'laboratory', and to the innovative British director Joan Littlewood whose experimental company was known as 'Theatre Workshop'. This has come to mean an experimental approach in which actors engage in joint exploration of a play rather than follow the precise instructions of a director. 'Workshopping' a play has become an accepted part of modern theatre practice. We read, for example, that David Edgar's *Teendreams* was partially devised in workshops with the women's theatre company Monstrous Regiment and was then developed in further workshops eight years later. Barrie Keeffe explains that his play *A Mad World, My Masters* (1976) required an intensive workshop period when the actors researched and created a number of characters and received crash courses in conjuring and the art of the confidence trick. But the term 'workshop' also implies a simple space with none of the elaborate trappings of commercial theatre. We can use exactly the same approach to help us in the study of modern plays.

The suggestions I have made for workshop activities assume that you have similar access to an uncluttered but fairly small space in which you can work with other members of a class or tutorial group. It is perfectly possible, however, to carry out some of these ideas at home with one other person or even, if you have no alternative, on your own. The whole prospect of a drama workshop may, of course, horrify you; you may think that it's only for people who are 'good at acting' or like showing off; you may feel very inhibited or you may simply never have had any experience of this kind of thing before. Give yourself and this approach a chance.

I am assuming *no* previous experience on your part and no particular talent for acting, but I am also assuming that you are a serious student who actually wants to understand a play from all possible angles.

If you are to understand how a play works, it is important for you to grasp that the person who wrote it knew how the theatre works from the inside. They have often allowed their work to be shaped in rehearsal, have held firm views on acting styles and have known how actors work. They have often rebelled against the performance modes of their day and have sometimes had a particular performer in mind for a part when they wrote it. These are all good reasons for you to explore the text in practical situations, and these activities will help you in the most difficult aspect of drama study: concrete decisions. Take, for example, the way in which a character speaks a certain line in a play and another character reacts to it. In the privacy of your own room or read silently to yourself, that line could be 'spoken' in any one of a hundred different ways – you need never reach a final decision and you can leave the precise meaning 'open'. But once you have to speak that line aloud or hear someone else speak it in a workshop reading of a scene, a decision has to be made about precisely how that line should sound. You may then decide that the first rendering was wrong and in the experimental atmosphere of the workshop you can move towards a satisfactory decision. Once you try out a line in context, so many factors suddenly come into play. Perhaps the character has just run up some stairs, been standing on her feet all day, found himself in a dark room with the sound of a 'hoover' around him – all such factors will affect the speaking of every word. The way in which one character elects to speak one line will, in turn, affect another character's reaction to it, and you can only really 'react' as a character when you have listened to what has been said to you.

None of this will demand great acting skill on your part, but it will demand concentration, imagination and a willingness to change your mind. Most modern plays are suitable for study in this way, because there are rarely more than a few characters on stage at a time and all the suggestions I have made can be applied to any play you are studying. The basis of many workshop situations is improvisation: that is, acting which does not arise directly from speaking a text. Many students are now acquiring experience in improvisation and appreciating its significance, but don't be daunted by this: if you are interested in any aspect of living, you will find you can improvise – after all, that is what most of us do most of the time, isn't it?

It might be helpful here if we group together the various suggestions I have made under a number of headings. I will then explain a little more about the approach to each of these topics and provide some examples. It is important for you to realise that, following the principles I have laid down, you can devise your own workshop activities to suit the needs of the plays you are studying.

▶ The play: words, actions and stage directions

Many useful workshop activities can be devised from the stage directions of plays because these establish the conventions for performance. I have already provided some examples in earlier chapters. Take the stage directions of any play you are studying and work through them together. Notice that they may tell you:

- Where and when the play is taking place
- Details of the way the play might be staged
- Where the characters move and how they look, behave or speak

Notice also that the stage directions will help us understand the motivation of the characters, that is, why they do what they do.

I suggest that you take as examples David Edgar's *Mary Barnes* (1979), Ibsen's *Ghosts* (1881), Debbie Horsefield's *Red Devils* (1981) or Sarah Kane's *Blasted* (1995). Use only a few pages and work through them together, pausing to discuss any issues.

▶ The play: characters and situations

The object of activities that I am grouping under this heading is to deepen your understanding of the characters in a play. You should always remember that what we call a 'character' begins as nothing more than some words and instructions on a page. Through imagination the actor converts this information into a living being. During exercises of the kind I am about to describe you will come to see more of the information supplied by the playwright and will discover what happens when an actor takes this material and begins to shape it into a performance. Here are two sample activities and you will find several others throughout the book:

- Ideally, work in pairs on this exercise. Select two characters from your set play who enter the stage and meet early on in the action so that this is the first time the audience will have seen either of them. Discuss the nature of this meeting – where and when it takes place, how long it is since the characters last met. Then, after acting out this moment, select another moment from the play when the two characters make their entrance and are seen on the stage together. Now take a character each and in your own words tell the other character what you had been doing before you met. Check the text for details and discover how much you have to present.
- Carrying the previous experience forward, make each character say aloud what they are actually thinking: this is the 'sub-text' – the real intentions and motivations that lie behind the words – coming to the surface. Now take the text of the play and work on the first meeting of the characters.

Use the first few lines of dialogue and all the stage directions and try this moment in various ways until you are satisfied that the relationship between the text and the sub-text and between the two characters is what you really feel the playwright intended. At this stage pairs may wish to come together for a discussion of what has been discovered and it is important to learn from each other's experience.

▶ Exploring the protagonist's journey

This category of activity can be quite lengthy and may well extend over several sessions and be expanded into a full workshop production. It derives from the fact that in almost every modern play the protagonist is involved in some kind of moral, intellectual or emotional journey. Tracing the stages in such a journey enables us to understand the depth of the play, so here is a sample approach:

• Begin with a group discussion. Ideally the group(s) should consist of as many people as there are characters in the play, but an additional chairperson or someone who wishes to have a go at directing can always be accommodated. Now begin to select all the key moments from the play involving the protagonist. This will not only include moments when the protagonist is visible but will also involve moments when other characters speak about the protagonist. Select a member of the group to be the protagonist and identify important meetings that take place between them and other characters. Now begin to construct a short version of the entire play focusing on key moments in the life of the protagonist. If necessary, link the scenes and speeches with improvised dialogue or monologue. You will find suggestions for this kind of activity relating to various protagonists in modern plays at various points in this book.

▶ The actors: talking, moving and listening

I am going to base these activities on the work of two great directors who had significant things to say about acting. The first, Peter Brook, began his analysis of drama with definitions as basic as 'what is a stage?' and 'what is an actor?' We can use this to help us understand the relationship between some of the conventions of modern drama and the meaning of performance:

• Create a bare space in the centre of the room. Ask one of your group to sit in the space. What questions does this raise? The moment an actor enters the stage space we have the ingredients for drama: we wonder where they have come from, who they are, where they are going, what they are going to do and, above all, what is the significance of their actions and activities. Ask your 'actor' to move around and do various things – everything becomes a *sign*, telling us something about the actor and the situation. Now suggest to the actor that he or she sits perfectly still but looks around the space or stares in one direction – discuss the effect this creates. If you catch a glimpse of another member of the 'audience' moving or looking around, it has very little significance for you (notice the common root of the words 'sign' and 'significance'), but the moment an actor on stage does anything or does *not* do anything, this is some kind of sign and at once you start to question further. You may immediately recall the opening of *The Caretaker* with this in mind.

The next activity is drawn from the great director, Stanislavsky, who was particularly associated with the plays of Chekhov, a contemporary of Ibsen. Stanislavsky's work with actors remains the most influential approach to the interpretation of texts in the theatre, and it is well worth studying the way in which he set about bringing a play to life in his productions. His great concern for truthful portrayal of characters led him to consider the way in which people change according to circumstances. The circumstances in which a character may find him or herself are almost limitless. A character is surrounded by an *environment*, *events* and *other characters*, and it is the interaction with all these that creates the tension and interest in drama. Stanislavsky named this aspect of work on a text as 'the given circumstances'.

• A sample activity using 'the given circumstances' might be as follows. Take a scene from your play that involves characters entering a room. Arrange the stage space to represent the room, then take a character each and survey the room, speaking your thoughts aloud. Is the room familiar to you? Is it welcoming or hostile? Where have you just been? What is outside the room? Question each character about his or her reaction to the room and how he/she feels on entering and leaving it.
• Now turn your attention from the physical world enveloping a character to the social world. Select a scene with two characters and act it out. When you have done so, ask the following questions: What do I now know about the other character that I did not know before? What is the consequence of the fact that I may know nothing more than I did before? Has either of us been trying to hide anything? If so, what tactics were employed?

▶ The actors: characters and their inner lives

I was once working on a production of the play *Woyzek* by George Buchner with a very remarkable director. We had been rehearsing for some while in a workshop situation and the director was clearly not satisfied with the way in which the actor taking the part of the protagonist was approaching the role. In some exasperation the director said to him, 'I do not see the *inner life* of Woyzek, I just see Roger trying to be like Woyzek!' This anecdote can constantly remind us that the job of the actor is to find that 'inner life', and there are various activities that can help us achieve this level of understanding.

* In whatever activity you take part, try to 'get in role': that is, imagine yourself looking, thinking and sounding like the character you've chosen. Take on that character's past life in your imagination and think of his or her behaviour characteristics. Arrange your working space to include any essential pieces, such as chair or table, and try to imagine all the rest.
* Some playwrights go to great lengths to provide information about characters for the actors. It is well worth taking the time to look at an example. Take, for instance, George Bernard Shaw's play *Candida* (1895). At the opening of Act I, Shaw provides a very detailed description of the environment of a fine October morning in 1894 where the Rev. James Mavor Morell is sitting preparing for a day's work. Every single item in the room has significance: the books, the pictures on the wall, the typewriter, the documents and the style of the décor and furniture. Shaw also gives a sketch of the character of Mr Morell and describes not only his physical appearance, sound of voice, way of moving and manners but also his passions, enthusiasms, interests and habits. It is unusual for playwrights to provide quite this degree of detail, although Arthur Miller sometimes comes near to it, but it is a good exercise to explore the means by which other playwrights *do* convey such information to enable actors to find the inner lives of their characters.

▶ The stage: shaping the space through design

As we have seen, modern drama depends a great deal on the way in which the stage space is used. We have already begun to explore this aspect of modern drama and here are two more activities of a kind that will recur throughout the book and will provide you with some insights into this aspect of drama.

- *A stage.* Clear a space in the middle of the room and decide that this is the area in which action will take place. Define the area carefully: this is your 'stage'; anywhere outside it is not. Now place an object of furniture in the space. At once, this has significance – it is no longer just a chair or whatever; it stands for something else – maybe a chair in Willy Loman's house, maybe a throne. If you are able to focus a spotlight on it, it becomes even more significant, because the attention of the spectators is drawn towards it. At this point you are actually engaging in designing for the stage, albeit at a very rudimentary level. The extent to which you shape the space through design will make a considerable impact on the presentation of the play. You can add other items to the stage: you may be able to introduce a change of level in the form of a rostrum or set of steps; you may add small items such as books or newspapers. Anything in the empty space that we call the stage is a *symbol* – it stands for more than itself. Now select the opening scenes of two modern plays and decide how you might present them on the stage you have defined. Notice how easily the space can be transformed to represent anywhere you wish and how simply such features as the boundaries of a room or the presence of a window may be indicated.

- Here is an extract from a modern play. Read it very carefully and then discuss the problems of staging it:

The corner of the house which contains the round drawing-room also looks onto a side street which leads upstage. To the left of the entrance, on the ground floor, is a window with a mirror outside it set at an angle. As the curtain rises, the bells of several churches can be heard pealing in the distance. The doors of the house are open. A WOMAN *dressed in dark clothes is standing motionless on the staircase. The* CARETAKER'S WIFE *is cleaning the front step; then she polishes the brass on the front door, and waters the laurels. In a wheel chair by the pillar, the* OLD MAN *sits reading the paper. He has white hair, a white beard, and spectacles. The* MILKMAID *enters from the left, carrying bottles in a wire basket. She is in summer clothes, with brown shoes, black stockings and a white cap. She takes off the cap and hangs it on the fountain, wipes the sweat from her forehead, drinks from the cup, washes her hands and arranges her hair, using the water as a mirror. A steamship's bell rings, and the bass notes of an organ in a nearby church intermittently pierce the silence. After a few moments of this silence, when the* MILKMAID *has finished her toilet, the* STUDENT *enters from the left, sleepless and unshaven. He goes straight to the fountain. PAUSE.*

(Strindberg, *Plays: One*, trs. Michael Meyer, Methuen, 1976, p. 157)

At this point in the extract the dialogue begins. The whole text you have just read probably came as quite a shock to you. The stage directions seem to be so complex that they create a whole series of images without a word being spoken. When the dialogue does eventually start it appears to be of an almost dream-like nature and the general impression is of a form of theatrical entertainment that works through a combination of visual and verbal effects. There is also a great deal of detail relating to sounds and to the physical appearance of the characters, and it would not be difficult to believe that we were looking at the script of a film. In order to understand the requirements of a scene we need to remember that 'Upstage' refers to the part of the stage furthest away from the audience and 'Downstage' is the front of the stage. 'Stage left' is the left-hand side of the actors as they face the audience. All this, however, only makes sense if we realise that we are thinking of a Proscenium Stage. This play, *Ghost Sonata*, was written in 1907 by August Strindberg at a time when proscenium staging was virtually the only form of staging used in the European and American Theatre. The many stage directions, rather than adding essential information to the characters or story-line, tend to add to a sense of mystery, so that although we know what is going on in purely physical terms we are never too sure precisely what is happening. A play that uses a range of different effects to create meanings in this way is a characteristic of *Expressionism* in the Arts and it has the same relationship with realism in the theatre as does a dream with the reality of everyday life. Reality is deliberately distorted in order to make it more powerful. Edvard Munch's painting *The Scream* would be part of the same artistic movement.

▶ The stage: shaping the space through lighting

Another way in which the stage space can be shaped and the audience's perception manipulated is through the use of stage lighting. Since the invention of electric stage lighting the range of colour, intensity and control has become almost infinite, and playwrights have been quick to exploit this remarkable medium. Let us look at a good example taken from Ibsen's play *Ghosts*. The following extract comes from the last moments of the play in which a mother, Mrs Alving, has to accept that her son, Oswald, is dying from inherited venereal disease. Notice that even in this tiny extract we can begin to get some idea as to the character of Mrs Alving. We make these deductions from her behaviour and her response to the situation in which she finds herself. In many plays, like those of Ibsen, the nature of the characters gradually emerges from what they say and do and from what other characters say about them.

He sits in the armchair, which MRS ALVING *has moved over to the sofa. The day breaks. The lamp continues to burn on the table.*

MRS ALVING [*approaches him cautiously*]. Do you feel calm now?

OSWALD. Yes.

MRS ALVING [*leans over him*]. You've just imagined these dreadful things, Oswald. You've imagined it all. All this suffering has been too much for you. But now you shall rest. At home with your own mother, my own dear, blessed boy. Point at anything you want and you shall have it, just like when you were a little child. There, there. Now the attack is over. You see how easily it passed! Oh, I knew it! And, Oswald, do you see what a beautiful day we're going to have? Bright sunshine. Now you can really see your home.

She goes over to the table and puts out the lamp. The sun rises. The glacier and the snow-capped peaks in the background glitter in the morning light.

OSWALD [*sits in the armchair facing downstage, motionless, suddenly he says*] Mother, give me the sun.

MRS ALVING [*by the table, starts and looks at him*] What did you say?

OSWALD [*repeats dully and tonelessly*] The sun. The sun.

MRS ALVING [*goes over to him*]. Oswald, how are you feeling?

OSWALD *seems to shrink small in his chair. All his muscles go slack. His face is expressionless. His eyes stare emptily.*

(Ibsen, *Plays: One*, trs. Michael Meyer, Methuen, 1980, p. 97)

- Work through the extract given above, then obtain the entire play and take other scenes to work on noting how the playwright constantly uses qualities and features of light to intensify the drama.

▶ Readers' theatre

Unless you have had a great deal of time to spare, it is unlikely that you will have had the opportunity to learn a role for performance, in whole or part, and your work will either have been improvised or have taken the form of a reading. In an attempt to come nearer to the idea of performance, many teachers and students in the United States have realised the value of what is called Readers' Theatre. Fortunately, the popularity of this work has spread to other parts of the world. It is a carefully devised and rehearsed mode of presentation in which the words are read by a group of performers with close attention to characterisation, qualities of speech and oral interpretation. There is no physical action as such, although a great deal of thought goes into arranging the readers in an effective way: they may each sit on stools in a spotlight against a neutral background and might decide to dress in a simple, unifying manner, all in black, perhaps. In order to create an imagined performance in the minds of the audience, the readers will read not only the dialogue but also some, if not all, of the stage directions, and will ensure that all the music and sound effects are cued in at the appropriate time. The result can be quite remarkably stimulating and has a great deal in common with one of the most formative influences on contemporary playwrights, radio drama.

Checklist

Key topics covered in this chapter:

* The nature and value of workshop activities
* Devising your own workshop activities
* The nature of the activities suggested with each chapter
* Organising your own presentation of Readers' Theatre
* Ways of exploring the 'sub-text' of a play
* The role of design and technology in the staging of drama

5 Studying a Scene

Once we have established a number of broad, general features of a play, we are in a position to make a much more detailed examination of the text. In order to do this we need to break down the material into manageable units, and in most cases we can use the 'scene' as a natural division for this purpose. If you are accustomed to studying Shakespeare, you will probably think of a scene as being a section of the plot that takes place at a particular time and location, so that, when these change, the 'scene' also changes. However, when you come to study a modern play it is far more helpful to think of the scene in the way that dramatists of the Renaissance and Restoration periods did: that is, every time *a new character is introduced* there is also a new *scene.* A scene, therefore, as our basic unit, is a particular encounter between a set of characters or even an encounter between a single character and the audience.

Most modern plays are not printed in Acts and Scenes. They are either divided into Acts, with very obvious divisions into scenes that are not labelled as such, or they are printed in a succession of scenes without any suggestion of a division into Acts. Both Miller's *Death of a Salesman* and Pinter's *The Caretaker,* for example, are divided into Acts without numbered scenes, whereas the plays of Brecht, David Edgar and Caryl Churchill often consist of a series of scenes. Acts will usually fall naturally into scenes and it's a good idea to begin your detailed study of a text by identifying these small units. This will provide you with manageable chunks of the text to look at in order to focus your analysis.

To illustrate the process of close study I am going to take the first two pages from a famous play that dates from 1879, the early part of the 'modern' period when theatre technology had already reached a high level of sophistication and when many of the forces operating in middle-class society were very like those of today. Ibsen's *A Doll's House* concerns the apparently happy marriage between the attractive Nora and her husband Torvald, who has recently been promoted to a good position in a bank. Torvald is infatuated with Nora and treats her like a beautiful doll while maintaining a strict moral tone in his household. Unbeknown to him, Nora has borrowed money and forged her father's signature in order to pay for a holiday that her husband needed when he was seriously ill. Nora has secretly earned money to repay to a money-lender, Krogstad, who begins to blackmail Nora into pressing her husband to find him a post in the bank. Torvald's reaction to the discovery of Nora's intrigue reveals attitudes that Nora can no longer tolerate, particularly since she has now experienced a sense of independence by earning money in her own right. The marriage disintegrates.

A first reading of the play might enable you to spot that the play is concerned with a tension between freedom and restraint. There is a sense that family life is ordered by artificial and narrow codes. The object of your then looking in far greater depth at a particular scene is to fill out your impression and see how Ibsen brings the play to life. A good scene to start with is the first. We are told in the list of characters that Torvald Helmer is a lawyer and that Nora is his wife; the action takes place in the Helmers' apartment. We then have the following detailed description of the setting:

A comfortably and tastefully, but not expensively furnished room. Backstage right a door leads to the hall; backstage left, another door to HELMER's *study. Between these two doors stands a piano. In the middle of the left-hand wall is a door, with a window downstage of it. Near the window, a round table with armchairs and a small sofa. In the right-hand wall, slightly upstage, is a door; downstage of this, against the same wall, a stove lined with porcelain tiles, with a couple of armchairs and a rocking-chair in front of it. Between the stove and the side door is a small table. Engravings on the wall. A what-not with china and other bric-a-brac; a small bookcase with leather-bound books. A carpet on the floor; a fire in the stove. A winter day.*
(The translation used here is by Michael Meyer, as printed in Ibsen, *Plays: Two*, Methuen 1980, pp. 23–5)

Three features should strike you. First, what this room tells you about the Helmers. Ibsen is quite specific that the room is comfortably but *not* expensively furnished; clearly the Helmers enjoy a very adequate standard of living but they are not affluent. The playwright also indicates that they are people of some sensitivity by the taste with which the room is furnished. And we further learn that music and books play a part in their lives through the presence of the piano and leather-bound volumes. In real life we often make rapid judgements about people's social class, attitudes and tastes simply from the appearance of their homes, and in *A Doll's House* we can form a provisional opinion of Torvald and Nora Helmer before we meet either of them.

Secondly, however, you should have been struck by the clear attention to the detail of this environment. Were you to be responsible for a production of the play, you can imagine the trouble you would need to go to in order to comply with all these specifications: a round table, porcelain tiles, china on the what-not, a *real* fire in the stove, and so on. Every one of these details makes an important visual statement and a contribution to the action and is therefore as significant as the dialogue. The playwright has taken great care to place his characters in a particular environment with which they can interact.

Thirdly, you will notice reminders of the fact that the play is to take place on a stage in a theatre. The doors, windows and furniture are positioned to be viewed from an auditorium through a proscenium archway. Their precise locations are defined as upstage (i.e. towards the *back* of the stage), downstage (towards the *front*), or stage right (to the right of an actor when facing the audience) and stage left. Additionally, the need for a fire in the stove and the description of the time as a *Winter day* will remind you that such effects must be achieved through the skilled use of stage lighting – a device that was not available to writers of earlier periods.

If you are able to make these simple deductions from a paragraph of stage directions you are well on your way to reconstructing the performance imaginatively in your mind and refining your understanding of what I have termed 'the world of the play'. After the opening paragraph of stage setting, a second, shorter paragraph initiates the physical action of *A Doll's House* and gives detailed instructions to the performers:

A bell rings in the hall outside. After a moment we hear the front door being opened. NORA *enters the room humming contentedly to herself. She is wearing outdoor clothes and carrying a lot of parcels, which she puts down on the table right. She leaves the door to the hall open; through it, we can see a* PORTER *carrying a Christmas tree and a basket. He gives these to the* MAID *who has opened the door for them.*

The sound of the doorbell and of the door being opened is a necessary reminder of the life outside the room on stage. Many modern plays have their action confined to a single room and their subject-matter is, in one sense, domestic. But how the events in that room relate to the world outside is important too. At this stage, of course, we might not remember that *A Doll's House* begins with the opening of a door and Nora's cheerful entrance and ends with her fateful, final exit and the slamming of the same door. However, this point illustrates the way in which stage directions are an integral part of the fabric and structure of the play.

First appearances of characters are especially important and you should pay particular attention to these moments. Shaw, another influential modern dramatist, usually gives an extended word portrait of the principal characters as they make their first appearances, and, although Ibsen, Miller, Pinter, J. B. Priestley, John Osborne or Caryl Churchill do not go to quite these lengths, they all provide substantial material on which the actors can base their performances. Details of dress are, like décor, an extension of the personality, and Ibsen very quickly establishes the *mood* of the opening with his instructions for Nora.

A general feeling of optimism and light-heartedness pervades the opening moments of *A Doll's House* and Ibsen quickly explains one of the reasons – the approach of Christmas. With her first words, Nora reinforces a sense of suppressed excitement and this overflows into her generosity to the Porter, to whom she gives two and a half times as much as he had asked for. This tiny incident of the tipping of the Porter very soon acquires significance in the rest of the play as Nora's handling of money and her apparent recklessness become a serious issue: again, you might not notice this sort of detail immediately, but do remind yourself that even apparently trivial incidents do have importance and resonances in the play.

Ibsen follows the first snippet of dialogue with a further series of instructions for the actress playing Nora:

> NORA *closes the door. She continues to laugh happily to herself as she removes her coat, etc. She takes from her pocket a bag containing macaroons and eats a couple. Then she tiptoes across and listens at her husband's door.*

The optimistic, carefree mood continues; there is something almost child-like in Nora's behaviour. As she 'tiptoes' across to the door we, the audience, are not to know that it is her husband's study she is approaching, but the moment we hear Helmer's voice from inside the room, we form a judgement of the kind of relationship that exists between them. Like Nora's conduct, it all seems on the level of a game. Helmer refers playfully to Nora as his 'skylark' and his 'squirrel': this might remind you of the two main characters in John Osborne's *Look Back in Anger* who call each other 'squirrels' and 'bears'. It comes as no surprise when Nora hastily hides the macaroons like a naughty child and perhaps the description of her as a skylark tells us about the kind of performance she is giving. As many of my students do, you may react with some outrage at Torvald's attitude to his wife revealed in the next part of this scene. I might add here that I initially divided Act I of *A Doll's House* into smaller scenes and still found these too long to handle easily. So what I've done is to select a section of the first scene for close analysis. And that is the way to do it: divide the play into scenes, choose a scene for analysis, then, if necessary, take an extract from a scene for even closer discussion. The opening scene is always a good example to use because you will often find it crowded with helpful stage directions and pointers about the characters. You will then have a solid sense of the play on which you can then build by looking at other scenes. Now, let's turn to the dialogue between Nora and Helmer:

NORA. Hide that Christmas tree away, Helen. The children mustn't see it before I've decorated it this evening. [*To the* PORTER, *taking out her purse*] How much – ?

PORTER. A shilling.

NORA. Here's half a crown. No, keep it.

The PORTER *touches his cap and goes.* NORA *closes the door. She continues to laugh happily to herself as she removes her coat etc. She takes from her pocket a bag containing macaroons and eats a couple. Then she tiptoes across and listens at her husband's door.*

NORA. Yes, he's here. [*Starts humming again as she goes over to the table, right*].

HELMER. [*from his room*]. Is that my skylark humming out there?

NORA. [*opening some of the parcels*]. It is!

HELMER. Is that my squirrel rustling?

NORA. Yes!

HELMER. When did my squirrel come home?

NORA. Just now. [*Pops the bag of macaroons in her pocket and wipes her mouth*] Come out here, Torvald, and see what I've bought.

HELMER. You mustn't disturb me!

Short pause; then he opens the door and looks in, his pen in his hand.

HELMER. Bought, did you say? All that? Has my little squander-bird been overspending again?

NORA. Oh, Torvald, surely we can let ourselves go a little, this year! It's the first Christmas we don't have to scrape.

HELMER. Well, you know, we can't afford to be extravagant.

NORA. Oh yes, Torvald, we can be a little extravagant now. Can't we? Just a tiny bit? You've got a big salary now and you're going to make lots and lots of money.

HELMER. Next year, yes. But my new salary doesn't start 'till April.

NORA. Pooh; we can borrow 'till then.

HELMER. Nora! [*Goes over to her and takes her playfully by the ear*] What a little spendthrift you are! Suppose I were to borrow fifty pounds today, and you spent it all over Christmas, and then on New Year's Eve a tile fell off a roof onto my head –

NORA. [*puts her hand over his mouth*]. Oh, Torvald! Don't say such dreadful things!

HELMER. Yes, but suppose something like that did happen? What then?

NORA If anything as frightful as that happened, it wouldn't make much difference whether I was in debt or not.

HELMER. But what about the people I'd borrowed from?
NORA. Them? Who cares about them? They're strangers.
HELMER. Oh, Nora, Nora, how like a woman? No, but seriously, Nora, you
know how I feel about this. No debts! Never borrow! A home that is
founded on debts and borrowing can never be a place of freedom and
beauty. We two have stuck it out bravely up to now; and we shall continue to do so for the few weeks that remain.
NORA [goes over towards the stove]. Very well, Torvald, as you say.

So far we've looked at the setting of A Doll's House, at the instructions
Ibsen gives his performers and at the appearance of Nora and the opening
mood. Now we can look at how Ibsen shows Nora and Helmer together.
Helmer's first appearance is a carefully prepared entrance. Notice how precisely Ibsen envisages it in performance: the first rather bland remark from
inside the door, showing that, at best, he's only half listening; the pause and
then the entrance as he realises precisely what Nora has just said. The first
impression we have of Torvald is that he is working; he comes out with his
pen in his hand. He is obviously some kind of professional man who works
at home, and although the rest of his family may be relaxing he is working.
Did you notice how economically Ibsen tells us that there are children? The
husband and wife roles seem to be pretty clearly defined: loving, solid, rather
sombre husband; attractive, fluttering, rather irresponsible wife. It may be
possible to speak Torvald's lines 'tongue in cheek', but they do have a serious
edge to them. He is clearly concerned that there must not be extravagance,
and, after all, the audience has been shown clearly in the details of the setting
that the Helmers are not wealthy. They have also seen examples of Nora's
ways with money that Torvald has not seen.

Soon, however, the context of Nora's behaviour is established. Ibsen feeds
a vital piece of information into what could become a simple clash of the
personalities. This is a very sensitive domestic situation that is familiar in
middle-class society: the husband has got promotion. In anticipation of the
larger salary Nora feels able to relax what has obviously been a very tight
budget. It is invariably at such times as Christmas that the need to economise
and 'scrape' hits especially hard, so it is inevitable that Nora, who has probably borne the brunt of such economisings, should feel as she does. Torvald
appears to take a rather joyless but possibly more realistic view, and we can
see in the divergence of their attitudes a source of tension between the characters and a hint of their respective predicaments.

We should remember that at the time this play was written the attitude to
borrowing money was much more guarded than in our credit-card age,
although the pressures that such borrowing bring are probably no less acute
now. In Ibsen's day there was a stigma attached to any form of borrowing.

Nora's suggestion 'we can borrow 'til then' has a contemporary ring to it, but it also suggests a desire to break out of a restraint that has become tedious. Helmer, taking her by the ear as an authoritarian schoolmaster might do, obviously feels that Nora is too reckless, too unwilling to look to the future and too anxious to embrace the philosophy of 'live now, pay later'. His comment 'how like a woman' would be regarded as unacceptably sexist today but we must also remember that the concept of sexism was virtually unknown in Ibsen's day. Indeed, *A Doll's House* is regarded as one of the most important works that contributed to the cause of women's rights in the nineteenth century. Notice how Ibsen uses this moment to establish the social order that Nora already appears to threaten. Man is the provider, the planner for the future; there must be no debts; the home is the foundation of society, a place of beauty and freedom.

The unit of the scene we have been studying concludes with an important stage direction that changes the whole mood. There is a note of resignation in what Nora says, but you should ask yourself, why does she move over to the stove? This is where your engagement in workshop activities will illuminate the written text. Try acting this short scene for yourself and if you are playing the part of Nora you will soon discover why you feel you must move away from Torvald at this point. Nora's *motivation* for this activity is her unease and, possibly, her irritation. Something about Torvald's attitude and what he has said clearly upsets her. The actress playing Nora in a full-scale production will, of course, have knowledge of the entire play and will have discovered significant facts about Nora's past that actually contribute to her reaction at this moment. Your answer to the question 'why does Nora move to the stove?' would also be more complex if you knew the entire play and that is why I have suggested that you should have got to know the play in general terms *before* you attempt such detailed study. However, in some examination situations you may be required to comment in some detail on an extract from a play you have not read. In that case you are like a member of the audience who sees Nora move and must decide at that moment why she does. That small physical aspect of the performance introduces an unexpected element of tension into the scene; it not only changes the joyous mood of the opening, but also suggests that Nora could quickly tire of her game of skylarks, although at this point, she seems also to be making a gesture of submission to her authoritarian husband.

You may now be feeling overwhelmed by what I am expecting you to dig out from a short extract; and you may also feel somewhat confused that we have so far made little mention of the actual words of the play. Do be reassured: *you can* make the kind of deductions I have made provided that you think of the play as a totality; that is, something seen and acted and not just as dialogue. It *does* get much easier with experience and there *does* come a point when you need to focus specifically on the language. Before you reach that stage, however, there are some important matters concerning a short unit of scene on which you should reflect. The extract we have looked at here is about the right length for you to consider initially. If you look at all the physical actions in the scene, such as the moment when Nora puts the macaroons in her pocket, the moment when Torvald takes her playfully by the ear or when Nora moves over to the stove, you will notice that these are all key moments that mark a significant if small change of mood or reveal some fact or attitude. Spotting these key moments will soon come quite easily to you and will help you to determine the pattern of a scene such as this. Looking back over it now you can detect a definite shape in its construction. Put simply, the tension gradually rises from a totally relaxed to a somewhat edgy mood. You should now be able to identify the stages by which it rises – there are key moments when the pace of the scene slackens and quickens. The playwright gives us pauses, longer and shorter patches of dialogue and some music (Nora's humming), all of which create a particular mood and impression. We are also given a great deal of information. Coming at the opening of the play, this is part of the *exposition* in which the playwright lays out the situation from which we may expect a major complication to arise. It is quite remarkable just how much we do know after this couple of pages – you should feel that you have a very clear idea of what is going on here. Ibsen, and many of the modern playwrights who followed him, took great care with this aspect of their work and the result is that we are given profound insights into character.

Most modern plays lend themselves fairly easily to the sort of rational analysis I have offered here. For example, you could take the opening scene of J. B. Priestley's *An Inspector Calls*: this play was written in a week during 1944 when the end of the Second World War looked inevitable but it deals with events taking place shortly before the outbreak of the First World War. There are many powerful ironies in the play and, like Ibsen, Priestley provides detailed descriptions of the physical setting and the behaviour of the characters within it. The initial unit of Act I is devoted to the establishing of a scene of domestic happiness based on the power of Capitalism and the inevitability of progress through hard work. In more recent times we might describe this as a Thatcherite vision. Although the event is Sheila's engagement to Gerald there is little doubt that the dominant figure is the industrialist, Mr Birling, who radiates supreme confidence, a sense of his own rightness in all things and a satisfaction with his own achievements that, he feels, gives him the right to lecture anyone and dismiss anyone who questions his set of values as a 'crank'. Indeed, questioning is the last thing we anticipate at this stage although the audience has good reason to realise that Birling's confidence is ill-founded. There are also telling clues about the generation gap and some sickening references to social climbing. The opening scene is clearly divided into convenient units and all that I have mentioned so far is carefully packed into the moments before the entry of Goole, the Inspector. This entry is skilfully prepared by the dramatist so that the audience can have no true idea of what may unfold. From this point, through questioning, a whole series of issues emerges with the developing story. You might notice the following: (a) the idea of a chain of events, (b) concepts of personal responsibility and personal freedom, (c) the use of cheap labour and exploitation, (d) the false distinction between being 'respectable citizens' and 'criminals', (e) attempts to use power and money to influence events.

Some of these themes are used in a much more recent play by the British dramatist, Caryl Churchill. Her play *Fen* (1986) provides us with a very fascinating contrast for the idea of studying a scene as a unit. I am going to give you the text of three short scenes from the play and will then examine them in the light of all that we have learned so far. Here are the scenes:

Scene Five
VAL *and* FRANK *dance together. Old-fashioned, formal, romantic, happy.*

Scene Thirteen
FRANK *and* VAL
FRANK. What?
VAL. I wanted to see you.
FRANK. Why?
　Silence
　Coming back to me?
VAL. No.
FRANK. Then what? What?
　Silence
　I don't want to see you, Val.
VAL. No.
FRANK. Stay with me tonight.
　Silence
VAL. No.
FRANK. Please go away.

Scene Fifteen
VAL *and* FRANK
VAL. I was frightened.
FRANK. When?
VAL. When I left you.
FRANK. I was frightened when you came back.
VAL. Are you now?

FRANK. Thought of killing myself after you'd gone. Lucky I didn't.
VAL. What are you frightened of?
FRANK. Going mad. Heights. Beauty.
VAL. Lucky we live in a flat country.
(Caryl Churchill, *Softcops and Fen*, Methuen, 1986, pp. 61, 81, 84, 85)

These very short scenes may have taken you by surprise if you have been working on the plays of Ibsen, Miller, Priestley or Pinter even. However, this is where your knowledge of the *conventions* and varieties of modern drama will be so useful to you. If you were to analyse any TV soap, you would find that many of the scenes are, in fact, no longer than these and we can clearly see the influence of film and TV on the writing here. Obviously we need a little more information if we are to make much sense of these scenes and we can discover from the published edition that *Fen* was written after a workshop session in a village in East Anglia (a part of Britain known as the Fens) and was later developed by Joint Stock Theatre Company, a group that specialises in the development of plays through improvisation and work with the playwright. This play is concerned with the exploitation of agricultural workers and suggests that in many ways little has changed since the nineteenth century. The convention of staging is an open arena that can represent anywhere, so there is little scope for giving information through the décor. However, the playwright was certainly able to use lighting, as the very opening scene of the play specifies fog and growing darkness. The twenty-one scenes that make up the play are of variable length and I have chosen the three shortest. What they show is aspects of a relationship, and you should be able to define and explore the nature of that relationship through the very spare dialogue and the minimal stage directions. Compared with the plays of Miller, Shaw, or Ibsen, we are told very little about the characters, but in order to understand these three scenes we need to see what *has* been told us in earlier scenes. We first meet Val, who we are told is thirty, working in a row, potato-picking. She tells the supervisor that she must go home and is very evasive when asked why. In a later scene we see her leaving for London with her small nine-year-old daughter, and then apparently she changes her mind. The next scene is the tiny moment when we see her dancing with Frank. This scene is loaded with meaning concerning their relationship even though no word is spoken.

We first meet Frank, who is thirty, driving a tractor and talking to himself, complaining about his low wages and explaining that he now lives apart from his wife and children. Val interrupts Frank's reverie by telling him that she is about to leave for London and pleading with him to go with her.

You can see now how, in order to maximise your understanding of the three short scenes I have given you, you need to pick through the play to find supporting material. When you turn your attention to the two scenes containing dialogue, you will need to imagine them vividly in performance. Listen to the rhythms, feel the pauses, sense the tensions, imagine what is unspoken and explore what is actually happening. This is a wonderful example of what actors call the 'sub-text': so much more is being said than is actually being spoken. The only way to analyse scenes like this is to remember all we have said about the way drama works through predicaments, tensions and threats and then to see how these are hinted at in what the characters are struggling to say.

In order to reinforce and extend the points I have made in this chapter I am going to ask you to look with me at one more short scene from a modern play. The extract is taken from *Mules* by the British-born Afro-Caribbean playwright Winsome Pinnock. This play was originally commissioned by Clean Break Theatre Company in 1996. This company provides high-quality, original theatre for women prisoners and ex-offenders, and the play was performed in a workshop version in Los Angeles and in a more polished form at the Royal Court Theatre in London.

The main theme of *Mules* is the recruitment of vulnerable black women to become involved in illegal drug smuggling between Jamaica and Britain. It is a play in two Acts consisting of relatively short scenes that alternate between Jamaica and London. The scene printed below is Scene 6 and is one of the shortest in the play. Both Allie and Olu are young black women.

Scene Six
London. Street.
Allie sits on the ground. Olu enters. Allie covers her face with an item of
  clothing. A coin is tossed on-stage. Olu picks it up.
ALLIE. Please, Miss, spare some change for a cup of tea.
  Olu stands and watches Allie.
  Please Miss, just a few coppers.
OLU. Do I look as though I have spare change?
ALLIE. Please. I have nothing.
OLU. What makes you think that even if I could, that I would give my
  hard-earned cash to you?
ALLIE. I was mugged. My landlady chucked me out of her house because I
  couldn't afford the rent. I'm all alone in the city. I haven't eaten for two
  weeks. I'm not very good at begging.
OLU. And is that my fault? By the look of you, you are strong and healthy.
  Why don't you look for a job? The rest of us have to work very hard for
  our money. Do you think that we are going to squander it away on
  people like you? You make me sick. [*She starts to walk away.*]

ALLIE. Please. I used to be just like you, had a job, family. My skin was soft just like yours.

OLU. Look, I'd like to help you, but I have nothing myself. All I have are a few coppers. Even if I was to give you something, just think how bad that would be for both of us. You would feel humiliated and I would get caught up in the superiority of being the one who gave. We would both lose out. Listen, the best way I can help you is to let you find a way out of your problem by yourself. Believe me, in the long run this is the best way.

Olu starts to go. Allie calls after her.

ALLIE. Thank you for your kindness.

OLU. Don't demean yourself with thanks. I don't deserve them. [*She leaves.*]

(Winsome Pinnock, *Mules*, Faber & Faber, 1996, pp. 28–9)

This is the third scene in which we have seen Allie who has emerged as the play's protagonist. At first glance, this scene might appear to be the form of simple encounter that you might devise in a workshop and, almost certainly, this is how it was first created. However, this is a carefully crafted scene, the full significance of which only emerges when you consider it in relation to the previous two scenes in which Allie appears. In Scene 2, Allie has arrived at a bedsit in London with a small bag, apparently containing all her personal possessions. She pays the landlady from a thick wad of notes and claims to be working as a waitress. When the landlady leaves, Olu, a young Nigerian woman from another bedsit in the same house, comes to Allie's room and asks for money. Olu suspects that Allie has run away from home and admits that she herself has done so and has been involved in drug smuggling. Allie refuses to give her money and when Rose, the landlady, returns they both send Olu away with insults.

In Scene 4 we see Allie with two other girls who have found her sitting depressed in a café. Allie admits she has no job and almost no money. The two girls, Pepper and Piglet, give her drink laced with drugs and she falls unconscious. The girls then rob her of her remaining money and some simple jewellery.

We can see, then, that Scene 6 is the lowest point yet in a downward spiral for Allie and the scene relates directly to the main theme of the play because she is now at her most vulnerable. All her initial sense of freedom, hope and optimism has given way to desolation: her predicament is all too obvious.

Notice how the scene begins. We, the audience, know that Allie and Olu had a previous encounter, but from this moment onwards their roles are reversed. By covering her face Allie gives herself a chance not to be recognised yet both characters continue to play the scene as if they had never met before. Examine the stage directions very carefully and observe how the dramatist builds her scene. The coin 'tossed on stage' that Olu picks up reminds us that Olu was penniless when we last saw her but also emphasises the casual and almost embarrassed way in which we respond to begging. We do not know if Olu has acquired any money since we last saw her, but she now adopts all the predictable and conventional reactions towards begging that we have all encountered. She establishes her power and superiority in the pause during which she simply watches Allie and then in the conversation that follows. Allie seems to be incapable of listening. Neither character actually listens to the other; they simply speak a personal script they have written for themselves.

We learn some important information from this short scene: Allie is now homeless. But the main effect of this scene is achieved through irony. Not only are the situations reversed from Scene 2, there is also a reversal of language. In Scene 2 it is Olu who says 'My skin was soft just like yours' and begs Allie to give her some moisturising cream, and the whole tone of Allie's and Olu's language has reversed. Olu, in fact, is playing an entirely different role here and has acquired the language to go with it. After some poignant moments earlier in the scene it is the final three speeches that are key to the whole play because they examine the way in which human beings demean themselves. Allie has gone beyond the point where she is capable of rationality whereas Olu voices the dilemma of the idea of charity for the giver and receiver.

The final irony in the lives of these two characters is that Olu, who appears articulate and able to discern a way out of a descent into destruction, dies transporting drugs inside her body, whereas Allie, who still has further to fall, finally ends up in prison where she has visions of a free soul.

You can see, then, that this very brief scene is, in some ways, a pivotal moment in the play and it is one of those moments that lingers long after it has passed. It is also a scene that wrestles with one of the most complex and alarming aspects of contemporary society.

In taking a short scene for your analysis you should notice how each scene you study relates to the next. In a play by Brecht the relationship may be undefined, very clear or minimal; in an Ibsen play the action of an entire Act is likely to be continuous and each Act separated by a clearly defined lapse of time. Observe the complete time span of a play and how that relates to the real time that a performance would occupy and the contribution of each scene to the whole. Playwrights' intentions will dictate their use of time, so that, for instance, Brecht will present events so that they do not seem causally linked whereas Ibsen shows the present as inextricably bound up with the past. Caryl Churchill often mixes characters from different periods of history so that in *Fen* a nineteenth-century child appears at intervals in a play largely taking place in the 1980s. The interest that the audience takes in accounting for characters' behaviour with reference to their past experiences is sometimes frustrated, as it is in *The Caretaker* or *Waiting for Godot*. In these plays the past seems threatening, painful but often hazy. Memory, that is so vivid in *The Glass Menagerie* or *Death of a Salesman*, becomes unreliable, so that both time past and time future are very uncertain, if not meaningless.

We have looked at the detail contained in a scene without closely considering the nature of the language that the playwright has created for characters to speak. Obviously, our account of a play is not going to stand up unless we do look at its language and focus on its detail. Once you have thought carefully about the action and shape of a scene you should then turn your attention to the language; this will constitute a further stage of your study of the play and will be the topic of the next chapter.

Checklist

Key topics covered in this chapter:

- Suitable units for study
- What is meant by a 'scene'
- Analysing a short scene in a rational and methodical manner
- Relating your study of a single scene to an entire play
- The motivation of characters and their world
- The variety of uses of scenes in modern drama

▶ Workshop activities

1. Devise an improvised scene in which Nora explains to a friend what living with Torvald is actually like.
2. Using the extract provided, find ways of acting the opening moments of *A Doll's House* and work particularly on the shifting relationship between the two characters.
3. Repeat this way of working on the three extracts from *Fen*.

6 Looking at the Language of Plays

We have already started to consider the language used in plays when we think about the conventions being used by the playwright. Now we need to explore this subject in more detail. Plays normally consist of people doing and saying things in a fashion that is carefully contrived by the dramatist. If a play were simply to consist of action with no speech or speech without action, we should probably find it unsatisfactory, although there *are* modern plays that experiment with both these possibilities. Some of Samuel Beckett's plays, for instance, consist of characters who speak but are entirely static, whereas Anthony Shaffer's play *Murderer* (1970) begins with half an hour of silent action. The kind of performance we now know as 'physical theatre', of which the company Théâtre de Complicité has become a brilliant exponent, also appears to break all the rules of theatre language. However, the fact remains that we normally expect the action and the dialogue of a play to be interrelated, one advancing the other. In some older forms of drama, both action and language were highly stylised and there have been experiments in recent times to follow this model, but the majority of modern plays rely for their effect on a mode of behaving and speaking that the audience immediately recognises as being like that of everyday life. This has especially been the case since Ibsen abandoned writing plays in verse in favour of what he called 'the very much more difficult art of writing the genuine plain language spoken in real life'.

To suggest that playwrights since Ibsen have merely attempted to imitate everyday speech is an over-simplification, for, clearly, just to use everyday language would be tedious, trivial and lacking in any form of dramatic interest. A playwright is not engaged in pure imitation but, rather like a TV comic who impersonates famous people, the dramatist takes certain characteristics and uses them in such a way that everyone believes in the likeness. In your study of a play you will need to be aware of some of the qualities of language upon which the dramatist has based the dialogue. In order to get to grips with this question of the language of the play I would suggest that you start by taking a very short extract as a sample and consider the following four points. It is helpful to keep a checklist of what you discover as you progress.

- Language and themes
- Language and character
- Language, thought and action
- Language and reality

▶ **Language and themes**

The dramatist's language serves to bring the play's action to life just as it also serves to bring the characters to life and to create a sense of the world they inhabit. I shall expand on all of these areas later, but the point I want to stress here is, in a way, much more obvious. What students sometimes fail to grasp is that the language of a play also serves to bring the play's themes to life. When you look at a scene or an extract from a play, you should be able to make a connection between the words spoken and the themes or issues that your initial analysis and reading of the play have established as important. For example, in an earlier chapter I suggested how an initial reading of *Death of a Salesman* might lead us towards seeing how the play is concerned with the gap between social harmony and the painful reality of life where men such as Willy Loman battle with failure. If you were studying Miller's play you would, by this stage of your analysis, have looked at a number of scenes to establish how Miller presents this large theme and creates his powerful, moving drama. But your analysis might remain rather vague unless you had also turned to the play's language to examine how it serves to voice Miller's theme. In the workshop activities of this chapter I shall be using a 'key' speech from the play *Pack of Lies* (1983) by Hugh Whitemore and you will see there how this point is emphasised. In order to illustrate the link between language and larger themes I am now going to introduce you to an example from Brecht's *Mother Courage and her Children* (first seen in Britain in 1955). We shall see the influence of Brecht in *Pack of Lies*.

In *Mother Courage* we see a woman and her children making their way across Europe during the Thirty Years' War, with the woman making her living by selling provisions to the opposing armies. Even without any more detail than this, you should be able to begin to see how the short extract below (from Scene 4) serves to illustrate the play's theme of war. As with all such extracts, the best way to gain an insight into how the language works is to bear in mind the idea of a tension or contrast between an idea of order and the reality of life's disorder, or between an idea of something positive and something negative. This contrast will provide you with a link between the play as a whole and the detail of its language. Here, then, is the extract:

THE CLERK. I know you. You had a paymaster from the Lutherans with you, what was in hiding. I'd not complain if I were you.

MOTHER COURAGE. But I got a complaint to make. I'm innocent, would look as how I'd a bad conscience if I let this pass. Slashed everything in me cart to pieces with their sabres, they did, then wanted I should pay five taler fine for nowt, I tell you, nowt.

CLERK. Take my tip, better shut up. We're short of canteens, so we let you go on trading, specially if you got a bad conscience and pay a fine now and then.

MOTHER COURAGE. I got a complaint.

CLERK. Have it your own way. Then you must wait till the captain's free.

(tr. John Willet, Methuen, 1980, p. 43)

Mother Courage is waiting outside the captain's tent to complain about damage to her cart. In that detail alone, in her words about how the soldiers 'Slashed everything in me cart to pieces', we get a sense of the horrifying violence of war and its wanton destructiveness. Clearly, this is the negative side of the scene and it's not hard to see how these details help to create a sense of the chaos of war. What, though, can we set against this idea? We should, I've said, be able to spot some sort of tension in the scene. Well, Mother Courage wants justice: she talks about being innocent, about having a 'conscience'. If you think about this, you should be able to see how the scene turns upon the contrast between the idea of the chaos of war and the idea of an ordered society where justice and innocence prevail. In the play itself such a scheme of things is shown to be remote – society is too busy making war and making money to bother about justice and innocence – but it is scenes such as this that bring these ideas to life. Of course, the language of any scene operates on several levels at once, so that besides bringing the themes to life it also brings the characters to life, which leads me on to the next point.

▶ Language and character

When we speak of a 'character' in a play we think of them as a living person, but, in reality, until an actor begins to work on the play the character is nothing more than a series of speeches and stage directions on the page. What a character says and how he or she says it are major features of bringing a play to life and will determine the way in which a performer conceives the person he or she is portraying. In everyday life we associate people with particular characteristics of speech, such as a tendency to talk a lot or to use certain peculiar phrases. The same applies to plays, and your first task in a study of dialogue is to *try and identify the speech characteristics of each character.* Look at almost any page of Tennessee Williams's disturbing play *A Streetcar Named Desire* (1947) where the character of Blanche DuBois is on stage and you will find that she does most of the talking. As we witness this volatile woman's progressive disintegration throughout the play, we are constantly aware that her patterns of speech dominate the stage and continuously draw attention to herself. Another play of which we might say almost the same thing of the central character is Osborne's *Look Back in Anger.* Jimmy Porter, the protagonist, is, like Blanche DuBois, one of the most memorable creations of the twentieth-century theatre. In the first moment of the play, Jimmy complains to his wife, Alison, and their friend Cliff, 'You bet you weren't listening. Old Porter talks, and everyone turns over and goes to sleep'; but as the play progresses we begin to understand why. Jimmy, the archetypal 'angry young man', is exceedingly articulate and speaks with the fluency of a highly educated person, but he simply talks too much and talks *at* people rather than *to* them. However, we only begin to understand his character and that of Blanche DuBois when we appreciate the frustration of not finding an audience who will listen. Pinter's *The Caretaker* is also, as we have seen, another play in which people do not listen to each other, although here the characters have quite different characteristics.

Where characters spend a great deal of time in conversation, as in Tom Stoppard's *Rosencrantz and Guildenstern are Dead* (1967) or Beckett's *Waiting for Godot* (1952), it is particularly important, though sometimes difficult, to notice how the characters are differentiated in the dialogue. If you get into the habit of reading the plays aloud and in engaging with workshop activities, you will, however, be able to detect the varying vocabulary, patterns and rhythms that characterise one person rather than another. Watch out for characters who invariably speak in monosyllables or in short, staccato phrases; others may use long, rounded sentences, and others will never finish a sentence or will punctuate their dialogue with pauses, 'ers' and 'ums'. This is where similarities to everyday speech are fascinating and crucial, because in spoken language we rarely use the complete sentences we would write. Many aspiring playwrights make this mistake and give their characters the kind of spoken sentences you would find in an essay, and the results seem highly contrived and artificial. That is the difference between a 'speech' which might be written down and delivered on some formal occasion and a 'speech' from a play which represents somebody talking spontaneously.

In everyday situations we frequently make judgements on people from the way they speak, and part of the process of studying the language of a play involves us in determining not only what judgements we have formed from a particular character's use of language but also what judgements other characters in the play would have formed. Under this heading, therefore, you will be looking for clues to educational and class background, place of origin, attitudes, level of confidence, self-esteem, skill in communication, ability to calm, persuade or influence other people and so on. Eventually you will discover that each character has his or her distinctive 'voice' and that much of the important differentiation between characters is achieved through language. You should make a note of all these features as they occur to you.

▶ Language, thought and action

When you examine the characters of a play it is useful to think of them as adopting various strategies to achieve certain goals. Insights into the motives of characters are provided by the words they speak. David Mamet's play *Oleanna* (1992) provides a worrying insight into the way in which people can destroy each other. In this play a student sets about the task of demolishing the character and reputation of her English professor. The opening moments of the play are preparatory to this unfolding drama: the characters appear to verbally circle around each other, each eyeing up their opponent but not revealing what their real intentions are. It seems, in fact, that the characters use language for everything *except* communication: it becomes a sophisticated form of defence system. So, the next stage in your study of a character's language is to *identify the purpose for which language is being used.*

In order to do this you should go back to the section on conventions in Chapter 2 and re-read my paragraphs dealing with conventions of language. Having done this, you need to think about the way in which language is *normally* used. We often use words to express our thoughts, but sometimes to conceal our thoughts. We may speak in an attempt to establish a relationship or to hide the fact that we are feeling awkward. We may say precisely the opposite of what we feel in order to achieve our ends. At times we will resort to polite formalities, jargon or jokes, whereas at other times it may be so important to us to say what we are thinking that we have to prepare ourselves, and even then, perhaps, not really say what we wanted to. We may flatter, sulk, talk excessively, lie, behave charmingly or rudely, all to achieve our own ends. Plays that deal with the issues of modern life are bound to use some of these characteristics of language.

Because there is the possibility of a discrepancy between a character's stated ideas and his or her true intentions, actors often describe the words of a play as the text and the motives behind the words as the subtext. You, as a student, are forced to be like an actor: to study the text in order to discover the subtext. The idea that something is going on all the time beneath the text is particularly helpful, and you should also bear it in mind when considering the silence that characters employ between speeches. When you are reading a play it is all too easy to forget that the characters carry on thinking and reacting when they are not speaking, and indeed, if they do not speak for some time, it is easy to forget their existence altogether! It is part of your imaginative reconstruction of the play in performance to consider how characters are using periods of personal silence. Think back now to those short scenes from *Fen*. What precisely is going on during the many silences between the words spoken?

Pinter's plays are particularly notable for the pauses that occur between speeches. A great deal has been written concerning Pinter's use of silence, and there is no doubt that in the theatre the intermittent silences have a stunning effect. However, the pauses are more than theatrical silence; they are often an indication that although two or more people are speaking they are not communicating. Whereas we normally expect a speech to be a response to a preceding speech by someone else, Pinter's characters often appear to talk along a line of thought governed only by themselves, and the pauses are either a non-response to a previous speech or a period of silent thought preceding another statement. Because plays usually consist of constant dialogue, silence can seem ominous and threatening. In Pinter's plays *One for the Road* (1984) and *Mountain Language* (1990) characters use silence to threaten each other, often in the form of an interrogation that allows the listeners no chance to follow the questioner's line of thought. The two tramps who wait at a roadside in Beckett's *Waiting for Godot* appear to use language as a defence against some kind of ultimate silence and simply to pass the time. This contrasts interestingly with *The Caretaker*, with which the play has certain similarities in that Aston and Davies begin their pause-punctuated dialogue in the opening scene by groping towards establishing the basis of their relationship. It is as if each character is tentatively sending up balloons and waiting to see if the other will shoot them down.

You ought to be able to recognise when characters are using language to overwhelm an opponent. Both Jimmy Porter, who taunts and attacks his wife in *Look Back in Anger*, and Mick, who terrifies the old tramp in *The Caretaker*, do this. They both have a better educational background or wider vocabulary than those with whom they share the stage and are more adroit and flexible in their employment of words. They can intimidate their fellow beings and dictate the whole style and pace of an encounter. Even when Jimmy is self-pitying, he still uses his weakness to focus attention on himself, whereas Mick simply confuses Davies, contradicting himself and deliberately introducing concepts he knows to be beyond Davies's experience. Jimmy enjoys the sound of language and cannot resist the ringing phrase even when he is close to desperation. Similar characteristics can be observed in the language of many of Pinter's characters and in those of Tennessee Williams, for example.

Conversation can be a very enjoyable activity and we often engage in it for its own sake. It is also the most common means by which we seek to establish relationships, impose our will on others and negotiate to achieve our aims. A play consisting entirely of pleasurable talk would be extremely boring because nothing would happen, but you will certainly find examples of *all* the possible uses of language in modern drama and invariably they will link with the thoughts of the characters and the actions they play. It is often said by critics that the language of a play should 'advance the action' and this is simply another way of saying that the dialogue has a great deal more than face value; it represents, for example, the major evidence for the protagonist's predicament. By the time you have studied several extracts carefully, you will have become used to recognising the purpose for which language is being used. You may, however, need to go back over earlier extracts to make sure that features you have now learned to detect have not passed unnoticed.

▶ Language and reality

Playwrights following Ibsen's example have been particularly interested in showing accurate representations of human behaviour, and this, inevitably, includes human language. More recently dramatists have been concerned to examine the apparent breakdown of language as an effective means of communication in modern life. This task appears to be all the more urgent with the ever-increasing opportunities for human beings to communicate through technology. All these areas of concern have led dramatists to provide dialogue that the audience recognises as having qualities of language used by people in the course of their everyday lives, including the use of telephones and computers. In studying a play you should ask *what features of real language are being highlighted*?

As we have already seen, the language of a play is carefully selected and shaped by the playwright, and by selecting certain features of 'real' dialogue it is possible to create the illusion of normal conversation. We readily accept, for example, that the characters in *Death of a Salesman* are conversing normally, yet if you examine almost any of Linda's speeches to her sons Happy and Biff in Act I you will find that they come near to poetry with their repeated patterns of consonants and strong rhythms. Miller has achieved the appearance of reality by using familiar vocabulary and sentence structure and by making Linda's speeches arise from and express her feelings in an entirely believable way.

Playwrights interested in the weaknesses of language as a means of communication tend to select particular idiosyncrasies of speech. In David Campton's play *Out of the Flying Pan* (1970) two delegates arrive from opposite sides of the world, one wearing blue, the other red. For the entire play they converse in high-sounding phrases arising from their ideologies, and although they are ostensibly discussing peace they actually never shift their ground because they do not listen to each other. Their substitute for genuine interaction is the language of diplomacy, a cunning verbal device that conceals real motives in a welter of impressive words. Campton seems to have taken almost all the diplomatic phrases that we might hear on the news or read in the newspaper and condensed them into a play that lasts about forty-five minutes. As with the most successful modern plays, the result is shocking, because through the dramatist's artifice we are made to see reality with a frightening clarity. A similar experience might result from seeing David Edgar's play *The Shape of the Table* (1990) that deals with the emergence of an Eastern European state into a democratic future. Negotiations take place between the old guard of Communism and the leaders of the new democratic state. But the shape of the table around which the talks take place becomes a cause of dispute.

What, however, are we to make of a modern play such as Eliot's *Murder in the Cathedral* (1935) in which the characters converse in poetry, some of which is so complex that its meaning is obscure at first hearing? It may seem almost perverse for a modern playwright to use poetry as dialogue, even if the subject-matter of the play is historical – after all, following *Murder in the Cathedral* Eliot went on to write several verse plays in which the physical setting was as contemporary as in a play by Ibsen or David Hare.

Eliot, however, argued that there were levels of reality. On one level a play may seem 'real' if the characters resemble everyday people, are placed in everyday settings, and speak everyday language, but for Eliot this was a surface reality dealing with trivialities and passing events that have little to do with eternal, profound realities. In order to cope with the universal and important truths and themes with which drama should deal, Eliot felt that the theatre demanded the elevated and richly textured language of poetry. If you are studying an Eliot play you will no doubt wish to discuss whether or not the playwright achieved a balance between language and action in his plays. Some critics and performers would maintain that by focusing entirely upon language, Eliot neglected other elements of drama, so that his plays are not entirely successful in the theatre.

Eliot and other playwrights who have experimented with the use of stage poetry are really not so far from Ibsen's great admirer, Arthur Miller, as it may first seem. It is misleading to think that there are simply two categories of theatre language: everyday prose and verse. We have already noted that at times the language of a play such as *Death of a Salesman* has poetic features, some of which help to establish a dreamlike quality of a play. Other modern playwrights have experimented with ritual language and carefully orchestrated speech that has strong poetic qualities while highlighting the stark reality of some of the action. Ann Jellicoe explored this approach in her terrifying portrayal of a world following a nuclear explosion, *The Rising Generation* (1960).

In their attempts to get closer to realism, British playwrights prior to 1969 felt frustrated and inhibited by the censorship laws, so it is worth checking the date of your 'set' play if it is written by a British playwright. The Lord Chamberlain was empowered to order the excision of any language considered indecent or profane before granting a play a licence for public performance. Playwrights argued that this prevented them from reproducing much of the vitality of the speech of large sections of the population about whom they wished to write; it was no longer acceptable to confine the subject of plays to the activities of the upper middle classes with their butlers, gardeners and parlour maids. With the abolition of censorship in 1969, many plays were, and continue to be, written with very accurate simulations of types of language that some people would consider obscene and shocking: Howard Brenton's play *The Romans in Britain* (1980) or Willy Russell's *Stags and Hens* (1979) would be good examples. What is really shocking about these plays, however, is the sheer emptiness and potential violence in the lives of the characters – characteristics that could not be portrayed so powerfully in all their awfulness without the language. If we are jolted into an awareness of something to which the dramatist wants to draw our attention, then the language has done its job.

The theatre may, simply through a pattern of language, bring us in touch with a whole cultural group with which we might be unfamiliar: Willy Russell evokes working-class Liverpool, Arnold Wesker and Caryl Churchill the life of rural Norfolk, Harold Pinter the East End of London, Arthur Miller modern and seventeenth-century New England, Conor McPherson rural Ireland, Charlotte Keatley modern Manchester or Dylan Thomas the life of West Wales. As you study a play you should be able to *identify the distinctive qualities of regional language* and relate them to the rhythm of life, the underlying outlook of the people and the cultural expectations of the characters. This requires that you develop an ear for language and that you listen with far greater attention than usual to all kinds of people talking. You can also benefit from participation in the suggested workshop activities. Listen to conversations in shops, takeaways, stations and other public places; listen to workers talking and the incessant patter of radio disc jockeys. Notice the way in which unsolicited telephone marketing people use language. How are all these people employing verbal skills? Are they just filling in time, joking, grumbling, enticing you to buy something you do not actually want? If modern drama is concerned with modern life, it is concerned with people such as these, and yet would anyone want to buy a theatre ticket merely to listen to such conversations? The distinction between a work of art and reality has always been debated, and you should be able to understand the difference between a play and a random 'slice of life'. The debate will become more complicated when you consider the huge audiences that appear to find the so-called reality of 'real life docu dramas' on TV gripping and rewarding!

▶ Key speeches

You have only to try writing a play to discover that there is a great deal more to drama than a succession of speeches, however memorable they may be. The fact remains, though, that the gradual unfolding of a play's ideas and action invariably depends on certain key speeches and that for many people the pleasure of going to the theatre includes remembering lines that linger in the memory long after the performance has ended. The aptness and power of much theatrical language makes it something to be savoured: the Inspector's dire warnings about the future in Priestley's play, Jimmy Porter's startling tirade against women in *Look Back in Anger*, Davies's account of his visit to the monastery in *The Caretaker*, Beatie's final outburst in Wesker's *Roots* (1959) or Laurence's sudden explosion of emotion in Mike Leigh's *Abigail's Party* (1979) are all still remembered by those who first heard them and they still make an impact. In some respects these examples show that the most effective dramatic language transcends the *dated* feeling of much modern drama written only a few years ago, but they show how great speeches *embody key concepts and mark an important moment* in a play. As a final suggestion for the study of a play's language I would recommend, therefore, that you *assemble a list of key speeches* and, if appropriate, memorise both the list and the speeches. Incidentally, a 'speech' may be just a few words.

As an example of this final point we might consider a couple of lines from Brenton's *The Romans in Britain*. The major theme of the play is the crime of occupation by one army into another nation's territory. Brenton creates a clever parallel between the Roman occupation of Britain and the occupation of Ireland by the English army. There is a moment when an Irish woman exclaims:

And how he thinks Ireland is a tragedy. Ireland's troubles are not a tragedy. They are the crimes his country has done mine. That he does to me by standing there.

(Howard Brenton, *The Romans in Briton*, Methuen, 1980, p. 101)

These few words directed at an English soldier appear to encapsulate the entire central theme of the play. At almost any point in your study a speech may strike you as being especially important, but the full significance of any speech cannot really be appreciated until you have a fair knowledge of the entire play. If you have followed the steps I have suggested in earlier chapters, this should not pose a problem now. In order to identify a key speech, ask yourself if it fulfils some or all of the following criteria:

- It appears to sum up or deal with some of the central ideas of the play
- It seems to mark a turning-point in the action so that you can trace events back to the moment of that speech
- It provokes particularly strong emotions in other characters and the audience – laughter, pity, surprise
- It reveals important aspects of a character's motives or attitudes
- It identifies the protagonist's predicament
- You tend to remember it without really trying

You might feel that it is impossible to apply these criteria because it is such a laborious business remembering them all or constantly checking speeches against the list. However, you will find that once you have grasped what are the basic characteristics of a key speech you will quickly acquire the skill of identifying them and explaining their importance. You will probably already have noticed that some of the criteria I have listed are so similar to one another that they are virtually indistinguishable, and this is because, in essence, whatever its precise nature, a key speech marks a *significant and identifiable step in the play's development*. Experienced actors and directors recognise such speeches almost instinctively, since they affect performance, and you need to imagine the effect that such a speech will have on other characters and on the audience.

I may have given you the impression that a play is, in effect, a series of key speeches linked by unimportant speeches. This is clearly not the case. Everything both seen and heard in the theatre has significance, though a play, like real life, in which every word and line had equal weight would not only be completely intolerable but would also rob the drama of essential heightening and relaxation of tension. If you carefully consider all the dialogue in a play lasting, say, two and a half hours, you will find that even the most apparently trivial remark has a purpose in the total drama, and that compared with two and a half hours of 'real life' the language of the play achieves considerably more in terms of interest, shaping events and mounting tension.

Identifying a few key speeches for special consideration as part of your study gives you the opportunity to look again at the general language characteristics of the play, but in greater detail. By the conclusion of your work on key speeches you should be able to comment in considerable depth on both the play's action and language in a way that will show a substantial advance on the earlier stages of your study.

▶ Analysing key speeches: a step-by-step guide, with examples

The total process now looks like this. Study the play in manageable units, a few pages at a time. Bearing in mind your knowledge of the whole play, select about six key speeches. If possible, choose speeches by more than one character, but also see that you have chosen more than one speech for the central character. Take the chosen speeches of each character in turn and apply all the questions we have considered in this chapter by using the following steps:

- Say in greater detail how the speech embodies a key concept or theme or marks an important moment in the play
- Examine the speech characteristics of the character
- Examine the purpose for which language is used
- Say what features of real language are being highlighted
- Read the speech aloud and say how the dramatist makes it effective

Obviously what I'm suggesting here is that, after you've selected your key speeches, you go through the same five basic steps with each speech. The workshop activities will be of particular help to you in tackling the final step.

I am now going to suppose that you are continuing to study Arthur Miller's *Death of a Salesman* and that you have reached the stage of selecting a number of key speeches. In order to give you practice and confidence in handling this task, we shall work through a sample speech. You will remember that Willy Loman, a travelling salesman, is desperately weary and unhappy in his job for which he is temperamentally unsuited. One of the major causes of tension in the play is the profound sense of disappointment that Willy feels in his sons Happy and Biff, for whom he had great hopes and ambitions. Linda, Willy's wife, reveals to Happy and Biff that their father, after working for his company for thirty years on a regular salary, has now been reduced to selling on straight commission, like a beginner. Money is now very tight. Biff exclaims, 'Those ungrateful bastards', and the speech I have chosen is Linda's reply. It comes about two-thirds of the way through Act I. I have studied the play in small units and this speech occurs in a section of four and a half pages in which Linda is talking with her sons. I have defined this section as a unit for study because, before and after it, Willy is on stage. The speech I have chosen is printed below. It is, in fact, the longest speech in the unit, but that does not necessarily make it the most important:

> LINDA. Are they any worse than his sons? When he brought them business, when he was young, they were glad to see him. But now his old friends, the old buyers that loved him so and always found some order to hand him in a pinch – they're all dead, retired. He used to be able to make six, seven calls a day in Boston. Now he takes the valises out of the car and puts them back and takes them out again and he's exhausted. Instead of walking he talks now. He drives seven hundred miles, and when he gets there no one knows him any more, no one welcomes him. And what goes through a man's mind, driving seven hundred miles home without having earned a cent? Why shouldn't he talk to himself? Why? When he has to go to Charley and borrow fifty dollars a week and pretend to me that it's his pay? How long can that go on? How long? You see what I'm sitting here and waiting for? And you tell me he has no character? The man who never worked a day but for your benefit? When does he get the medal for that? Is this his reward – to turn around at the age of sixty-three and find his sons, who he loved better than his life, one a philandering bum –
>
> (Penguin, 1961, p. 45)

1. *Say in greater detail how the speech embodies a key concept or theme or marks an important moment in the play.*

This speech tells us a great deal more about Willy's predicament than either Happy, Biff or the audience have previously understood and it also reveals far more about Linda. It provokes both surprise and pity and has the genuine ability to shock. It identifies the central issue of the play – the ruthlessness of the consumer society – and I find that it lingers in my mind. For the first time in the play, Linda expresses something of the depth and intensity of her affection for Willy and she is now desperately trying to make her sons appreciate the gravity of the situation and the inappropriateness of their attitudes.

What I think is also evident in this speech is the central tension that runs through the play as a whole: the tension between the idea of harmony and the painful realities of modern American life, or indeed of consumer society in general. Look at how few words in this speech suggest attractive, positive things – 'friends', 'loved' – and set these against the images of life as cruel and indifferent, such as the haunting image of Willy taking his cases out of the car and putting them back again 'exhausted', or the equally disturbing image of Willy driving hundreds of miles and 'no one welcomes him'. Again, look at how the speech contrasts the past as enjoyable and successful with the hollow and hopeless present where Willy has to pretend that he is still a great salesman. There is something unbearable about that present, as if there is nothing solid or worthwhile left in Willy's life. Your response to this speech may be very different from mine, but I hope you can see how, just by looking at a few details and relating them to the play's theme, my analysis has progressed and really started to investigate Miller's drama.

2. Examine the speech characteristics of the character

Linda tends to speak at greater length than the other characters and she is more reasoned and persuasive in her whole approach. She drives home her points by strong, simple vocabulary and compels people to listen to her. She gives the impression of pent-up energy; hers is 'educated' grammatical speech although she occasionally leaves phrases incomplete in her anxiety to make a point. Here you should think again of the speech and its context and of your experience in reading it aloud. Imagine how the speech is designed to be spoken – perhaps quickly, loudly, in agitation, excitedly, or in some other way; then imagine how Linda might move or stand as she speaks and imagine the effect of the entire speech in the theatre. Ask yourself how the speech of this character differs from that of other characters in the play.

3. Examine the purpose for which language is used

What Linda most wants is to change her sons' hideous attitudes, to shake them into a recognition of the truth and force them to confront the reality of the situation. She tries to do this by sharp questions and short, piercing statements. You need to read this speech aloud and explain *how* the dramatist makes it work: features to look for might include various forms of repetition, strongly accentuated words, or the use of alliteration (several words beginning with the same consonant) or assonance (recurring vowel sounds). All these techniques help to emphasise a point. Repetition usually achieves emphasis, but this may be of various kinds, and serve different purposes: for example, a character may be trying to drive home an important issue or express disbelief. Look also for questions or images that characters use to make their language more vivid. The tone of a speech, often determined by the use of irony, sarcasm and humour, gives a clue to its purpose.

4. Say what features of real language are being highlighted

Linda's speech has the energetic flow of a person who is angry and determined to persuade. There are many questions and these are characteristic of somebody trying to make a point strongly, yet the language is simple, everyday vocabulary. This is a mother talking to her sons, so there is a sense of common language between them; it is uncomplicated and domestic and yet it has the power of a public statement. There are no particular regional features except that both her description of her son as a 'philandering bum' and her expression 'in a pinch' are clearly East Coast American. To identify language features look particularly at the sentence *structure*. Are there single detached sentences containing just one or two words? Or are there long, complex sentences? Or are these used in combination? You might look also for the use of jargon and dialect here.

5. *Read the speech aloud and say how the dramatist makes it effective*

This is a strong speech built on contrasts – it begins with a surprise accusation of the sons and then compares what was once possible with what is now the case. There is a brittle quality in the alliteration of repeated *b* sounds – 'brought', 'business', 'buyers' – yet the sense of a more pleasant past is created by repetition of the word 'old' and the long vowel sounds of 'now', 'loved', 'found', 'order', and suddenly ended by 'dead'. Later in the speech Linda presses home her point with repeated 'why?' The contrast of past and present is achieved through striking acrimony which also creates a sense of false hope: 'he takes his valises out . . . puts them back . . . takes them out . . . Instead of walking he talks now' – here the hinted rhyme achieves further contrast and emphasis.

The second half of the speech takes the form of a series of questions of ever-increasing urgency. Linda concludes by rounding on her sons, with whom the speech began. As the speech progresses the sentences become shorter and more fragmented, building the tension, but they are all of relatively simple structure. The tone of the speech is almost rhetorical; it has the art of a public persuasive speech and it becomes increasingly bitter. There are moments of great pathos as Linda builds a picture of Willy's life and then moves on to the attack.

You can see that the logic of this final step in the analysis of a key speech is to bring together again the issues you have explored in the second, third and fourth steps. By doing this you will avoid ending up with a very bitty analysis. After reading the speech aloud and thinking about its effect, it's often a good idea to re-examine your response and also to think about the speech as spoken, the other characters' reactions and what happens afterwards. Or you might think further about the character's intentions in delivering the speech, or how it compares with the speeches of other characters. The following paragraphs give some of my own further thoughts about Linda's speech that have been formulated as a result of seeing the play performed and reading the speech aloud many times.

The speech gradually accelerates in pace and urgency and probably in volume. Linda may be on the point of breaking down as she reaches the end, but she gives the impression of great control at the start. The speech would be spoken in a calculated, almost icy way, but there is great emotion in it and this should not be far from the surface. It comes as a shock and we can imagine that it would be heard in silence with great attention – Linda's strength, as shown in this speech, is surprising and compels our listening. Only Happy and Biff are addressed and only they and the audience hear. The speech is a reply to Biff's comment on the ingratitude of Willy's employers but both Happy and Biff are indicted. Happy has shown a greater readiness to understand Willy's predicament than Biff but they both have no real conception of his suffering. Biff's reaction is aggressive, as if he is both unable and unwilling to accept the implications of what has been said. Happy makes a single exclamation, 'Mom!' (it is he whom Linda has dismissed as a 'philandering bum'), but he can make no further comment; he seems shocked, deep in thought and in a sense admits that there is no answer.

Linda's intention has been to shock her sons into confronting the gravity of Willy's predicament and she is partially successful. She stings them both into some kind of response, but Linda still has to tell her sons more before they finally realise the full truth. Beneath the text is Linda's lonely carrying of a tremendous burden, the fact of living out a lie, and she can no longer bear it. Thus her frustration and anger come to the surface in this speech. Unlike many of Linda's earlier speeches, in which we feel she is concealing her true feelings, on this occasion she says exactly what she means and retains sufficient control over herself to say it completely. Linda's speech is less colloquial than that of any other speaker; she uses language with greater sympathy and more control than Willy or her sons. Her words appear to be carefully chosen for maximum effect and they have a greater flow than any of the speeches of the other characters.

The speech itself demands action from Happy and Biff, and their subsequent attitudes and behaviour are shaped by it. In the short term Biff rejects the guilt and there is a growing tension of resentment between the two boys. The most immediate result of the speech is that Linda is forced to tell her sons that she has discovered that Willy is contemplating suicide.

I hope this example will show you the level of attention that you can bring to a key speech. My comments are by no means exhaustive and you may feel that I have missed something you would have mentioned. So much the better. You will notice that I have used all the steps I have suggested but within each step I have allowed myself considerable flexibility; you should feel free to use the steps as guides, not as narrow rules. Further exploration of the language of a play can be achieved in a practical workshop situation. It's likely that thinking about the dramatist's words in the way I have outlined is a new experience for you, and inevitably it will seem very time-consuming at first. Time spent at this stage, though, will equip you to approach your study with much greater confidence in the future and you will find yourself asking many of the questions almost unconsciously before long.

Checklist

Key topics covered in this chapter:

- The relationship between language and the themes of a play
- The links between language and character
- How language, thought and action are linked
- The relationship between the language of a play and reality
- Identifying the characteristics of a 'key speech'
- Analysis of a key speech using five simple steps

▶ Workshop activities

1. Here is a speech from the play *Pack of Lies* by Hugh Whitemore. This play tells the story of Bob and Barbara, a couple in their forties who live in a comfortable London suburb during 1960. They and their teenage daughter, Julie, become very friendly with some new neighbours who have moved into the house opposite, Helen and Peter. Some while after their friendship has developed they are astounded to receive a request from the police to mount a surveillance operation from their house and eventually Peter and Helen are arrested for spying for the Soviet Union. The devastating effect on Bob and Barbara is eventually the main thrust of the play. Here is the opening speech:

    BOB [*Enters and addresses the audience*]. I was out in the garden when I heard the doorbell. It was a Saturday afternoon. I was just pottering about, sweeping up leaves and so on. Barbara and Julie had gone shopping. When I opened the front door I found a man and a woman smiling at me. They were holding a Bible and some religious pamphlets. 'We've come to bring you the key to great happiness' the man said. 'Thanks very much,' I said, 'but I'm happy enough as it is' – and shut the door quickly before they had a chance to say another word. They walked away slowly, still smiling – I could see them through the window. I suppose they were used to having doors slammed in their faces. Later, when I was back in the garden I thought to myself, 'Well, it's true – I am happy – it's true.' And for a moment I stood there, grinning from ear to ear, just because I felt happy for no particular reason. [*He grins*]. It was marvellous.

(Hugh Whitemore, *Pack of Lies*, Amber Lane, 1983, p. 11)

Work in pairs or as a group on this speech and apply step five from this chapter to this speech. When you have done this and discussed the effectiveness of this speech, discuss the four other steps we have dealt with in relation to this speech.

2. Devise some improvised scenes that might take place in this play. Use my brief summary of the action as a basis but feel free to invent incidents of your own. Remember that the events of this play actually happened and took place at the height of the Cold War. Peter and Helen Kruger were two of the most notorious spies at this time and were both Canadian.

3. Improvise some scenes in which you adopt the language characteristics of someone you know well. Then contrive some meetings between the various characters you have created.

7 Tackling Different Kinds of Play

All the steps that I have suggested so far in your study can be applied to any play, but there comes a stage when you are bound to realise that the particular play you are studying has certain labels and definitions attached to it and that it has characteristics that make it like some other modern plays and unlike others. The difficulty of categorising plays in modern drama stems from the fact that they belong to a period of great experimentation and will include works of every imaginable shape and form, lasting anything from thirty seconds to several days. Nevertheless, despite this variety, modern plays are often grouped into categories and almost certainly you will want and need to become familiar with various terms of reference if you are to discuss the plays in the light of what has been said about them. More important still, you will need to make sure that you are studying and evaluating a play in a manner that is appropriate to its type. We can easily find ourselves asking entirely the wrong questions about a play if we have failed to spot what sort of play it is. It's rather like judging a soccer match as if it was a game of tennis – you end up in the wrong ball game! For example, some modern plays can be maddeningly obscure. In Pinter's *The Birthday Party* (1958) we never discover the true identity of two men who come to a seedy seaside boarding-house and take away a third man; but it's no good writing a criticism of this play as if it was a play by Shaw or Arthur Miller where a brief biography of each character appears in the text and a satisfactory resolution emerges at the end. If Pinter's play *was* like that, it would cease to have the qualities that make it so powerful. Similarly, we cannot evaluate a play by Brecht or one of the playwrights influenced by him as if it was written by Ibsen.

The next step, then, is to decide what kind of play we have been studying. This may seem rather a late stage at which to make this decision, but it is only now that you have sufficient detail to make such an informed decision. Before we look at some possible categories and definitions, you must remember that any one play can fit several categories and that no label is a complete description of any play. Another preliminary is to tackle two terms that have become very widely used in the study of modern drama but are very tricky to define: *naturalism* and *realism*. The problem is that the two terms are often used nowadays as if they were synonymous, and, frankly, a great deal of energy can be wasted in trying to find a difference between them. However, the two words had distinct origins as applied to drama, although both came into prominence in the latter half of the nineteenth century.

Realism describes a form of drama in which the dramatist shows us people behaving in recognisably human ways in settings that look like the real world we know. Ibsen contributed enormously to the development of realism in the theatre: he discarded 'asides', 'soliloquies' and other non-realistic devices and he was careful to give a purpose to any exposition. Often, a character who has just arrived elicits information in what seems a completely natural way, by asking questions. All the scenes have a causal link and lead logically to the *dénouement* – that is, a dramatic end, where the threads of the plot are drawn together and a resolution is reached. The characters, costumes, settings and activities are all chosen to reveal important information and are detailed in the stage directions; the characters are also shown to be heavily influenced both by heredity and by their environment and have complex psychological motivation for their behaviour.

Naturalism was a movement in the arts in late-nineteenth-century France. Taking the lead from recent work in the field of evolution and heredity, the naturalists insisted that all human behaviour was a product of heredity and environment and that therefore there was really no free choice. Art, they said, should reflect this and show human beings just as they are in their predicament. A naturalistic play must show the characters behaving as people would do, given the circumstances being shown, and there could be no carefully contrived *dénouement* or story-line. Naturalism was to reveal nature as it is: a play should be a 'slice of life' transferred to the stage and must present the same level of scientific truth as if the characters were being examined under a microscope.

There have probably been no great plays that truly satisfied the definition of naturalism, but perhaps some of Strindberg's plays come close. Many elements of naturalism are present in modern drama and the term is frequently applied to the style of acting that seems appropriate to the dramas of everyday life that form the bulk of the plays written by and since Ibsen. At this point, however, it may be helpful if we look at some of the broad categories and labels of modern drama.

▶ Well-made plays

The term 'well-made play' is also of nineteenth-century origin and was first used by the playwright Eugene Scribe (1791–1861), whose plays you are most unlikely to study. The well-made play has remained a popular formula with modern dramatists because it is such an effective means of introducing the sense of the breakdown of an established social order and a complex predicament facing the protagonist. A well-made play consists of three or four Acts. A group of people in a lifelike setting are in some way disturbed either by the arrival of a new character or by some unexpected occurrence; the characters are forced to regroup to bring about a satisfactory end. There is an initial period of careful *exposition* in which the ground is prepared; then a period of *complication*, in which information is withheld, incidents follow in a chain of cause and effect, startling reversals occur and suspense is created, often bringing scenes to a climax; and finally there is a bringing together of various strands and a resolution of the problems in a *dénouement*. Writers such as Ibsen, Chekhov, Shaw, Priestley, Orton and Ayckbourn have all used the formula of the well-made play with great effect because it provides a very satisfying theatrical experience, never allowing the audience to relax completely, yet moving towards a resolution that can form a talking-point after the play.

If you have identified the play you are studying as belonging to this type, here are a number of special steps you should add to those you have already carried out:

- Discover how the exposition of the play is handled
- Discover how each scene is brought to a climax by identifying the events that cause suspense
- Think about the manner and nature of the resolution of the plot in the denouement

Let's take each step and think about it more:

1. As you will recall, the well-made play is invariably realistic and the way in which the audience is provided with background information has to be subtle. In many plays, such as Ibsen's realistic plays, an old friend or a character from the past arrives and there is talk about the intervening years which reveals a lot about the people and their situation. Chekhov's play *The Cherry Orchard* (1903) opens with a group of people returning to an old family home, and so there is a period of excited reminiscence that prepares the ground for what is to come. To help yourself determine how the exposition is handled, stop every couple of pages and ask yourself what you now know that you didn't know before, and how you know it.
2. Peaks in the action can be represented on a diagram. Try drawing a graph showing where the climaxes occur; this will give you a feel for the shape

of the entire plot as well as insights into its complications. As the 'plot thickens', the protagonist's predicament becomes more intense, so this examination of the structure of the play will reinforce your earlier investigations into the nature of this predicament.

3. The *dénouement* will not only bring the story to an end but will resolve the predicament in some way. The resolution may not be happy – it may be death or someone walking out – but it will bring a sense of finality and may involve reconciliation or justice. You should detect how the strands are brought together and how the playwright keeps you in suspense by delaying certain revelations or events. You should also consider what set of ideas is challenged or confirmed by the *dénouement*.

▶ Problem or thesis plays

The description I have offered of a well-made play obviously suits the needs of thrillers, such as the plays of Agatha Christie or Frederick Knott, that are popular with amateur dramatic societies. However, a more profound form of drama was created out of the apparently straightforward formula of the well-made play by great dramatists such as Ibsen and Shaw. This is the 'problem play', a play that explores a particular social problem, raising many questions about it and provoking the audience into finding answers. Such plays, sometimes known as 'thesis plays' because they mount and work out an argument, may be tragic or comic in essence, but their ideas constitute some issue of deep concern to the dramatist with which he wishes to engage the minds and consciences of the audiences. The power of a problem play presented in the well-made format, is the contrast between the apparent logical simplicity of the form and the real complexity of the issue with which the play deals. When you are studying such a play you must aim to end up with a grasp of both, so after your initial analysis of the play, apply the following steps:

• Define all the factors that motivate the characters or in some way affect their behaviour
• Identify what decisions have to be made by the main characters and what moral/social issues are involved
• Try to detect the dramatist's stance towards the topic and state clearly in your notes where you feel matters are left open-ended
• Discover all you can about social conditions and moral attitudes pertaining at the time the play was written

Audiences have quite frequently been shocked by problem plays: Ibsen's *A Doll's House* and *Ghosts* were greeted with howls of protests. Someone described *Ghosts* as 'an open sewer' and a press review called it 'a dirty deed done in public'. In the same way, TV audiences in the late 1960s were so disturbed by the play *Cathy Come Home* that it led to the formation of the organisation 'Shelter' to care for the homeless. A more recent example of a play that shocked audiences was Brenton's *The Romans in Britain* and it led to a lawsuit under the obscenity act. Thus we can see that in order to fully understand a play we need the final step that I have mentioned.

Some authors, like Miller and Shaw, provide a preface to their plays explaining some of the issues with which they deal, and many play editors include a good, scholarly introduction that is useful in the same way. Editors will often include some evidence from other contemporary sources to illustrate why a particular issue was of special interest to the dramatist, so, for example, you will be in a far better position to study Ibsen's *A Doll's House* if you know something about nineteenth-century attitudes towards marriage. There are plenty of problem plays still being written as dramatists continue to attack society's laws, attitudes and injustices, and you will find it very fascinating to acquaint yourself with plays by such writers as David Mamet, Steve Gooch, David Edgar, Shirley Gee and Caryl Churchill.

▶ The new realism

Like all formulas, there *is* something predictable about the well-made play, and many playwrights, anxious to make their distinctive voices heard, have found it a restricting and outmoded form. In the process, of course, many fine dramatists like Terence Rattigan have suffered an undeserved period of neglect, but since the Second World War the most innovative and interesting dramatists have abandoned the well-made play and experimented with alternatives. This was partially due to the fact that in the hands of lesser imitators of Ibsen and Shaw, a form that was intended to convey reality had come to seem contrived and artificial. Writers such as Arthur Miller, John Osborne, Arnold Wesker or Shelagh Delaney were anxious to present aspects of the reality of everyday existence in new and striking ways. Their settings were equally realistic but sometimes showed a squalor or ordinariness unfamiliar to theatre audiences. Instead of elegant drawing rooms with drinks and cocktail cabinets, there were dingy tenements, bedsits and poorly furnished small houses, with drinks straight from the fridge. Instead of articulate and elegant conversation, such as one might find in a play by Noel Coward, there was language full of vigour and colour from the working-class tradition and from various regions. Such plays usually show people struggling against the pressures that society puts on them. This type of play is common in the work of dramatists like Caryl Churchill, John Godber and John McGrath, all of whom expose the grim reality of people's lives and working conditions. It was a terrifying example of the new realism that set in motion a train of events that culminated in the abolition of theatre censorship in Britain. Edward Bond's *Saved* (1965), that contained a scene in which a baby is stoned to death in its pram by a group of bored, unemployed youths, was originally refused a licence for public performance. The Royal Court Theatre was determined to present the play and created a private club in order to do so. This situation was recognised as farcical and the law on censorship was eventually repealed. Bond's play, like all his other work, was looking at the problems of our culture and presents a bleak picture of life and a warning that has not been heeded. The last scene of the play is remarkable in that it is an almost silent episode in the home: a husband doing the pools and the women sitting around and uncommunicative. Len, the lodger, is mending a broken chair; no one pays any attention when he asks for a hammer – these are the only words in the scene – and he finishes the job as best he can without a hammer.

Once you have completed studying your play using the various steps outlined so far, it would be helpful if you were able to do the following:

- Sum up why you think it was necessary for the dramatist to show social reality with such detail
- Ask yourself why the playwright has chosen *not* to write a traditional well-made play
- Ask yourself if the play is some form of protest

During the 1950s and 1960s, British plays that showed a realistic picture of life, in what were often fairly squalid conditions, were nicknamed 'kitchen sink' dramas. This somewhat dismissive description overlooked the fact that such plays were often written as a protest against the drabness and injustice of life. You should be able to detect the playwright's standpoint and understand the means chosen to confront the audience with the reality of other people's lives. Shirley Gee's play *Ask for the Moon* (1987) contrasts the appalling conditions endured by nineteenth-century lace workers with the equally shocking conditions of a modern sweatshop. Caryl Churchill's *Fen* uses a similar technique to highlight the plight of modern farm workers; so we can see that plays of protest were by no means confined to the 1950s and 1960s.

Not all plays that are set in rather drab, everyday surroundings are a protest – on the contrary, many show the warmth and vitality that exists in the most unpromising of conditions. In recent years, however, the kind of realism of the kitchen-sink drama has been taken up quite successfully by TV. You should not, however, confuse the entertainment offered over a prolonged period by the 'everyday' dramas of a soap with the altogether more intensive experience of seeing a play in a theatre. Soaps are just as cunningly constructed as a well-made play, each episode being carefully brought to a climax to ensure that you will watch the next. 'Real life', as we well know, does not consist of a series of well-ordered scenes – it would be much easier if it did; many people's lives are singularly uneventful and at times boring, so if a dramatist aims to show real life, all this must be shown too. You must decide how a playwright has *created* and *sustained* interest in the characters and their situations, however mundane they may be. In *Roots* (1959), a famous play by Arnold Wesker, we see a picture of the humdrum and monotonous lives of a family in rural Norfolk. For them, the passing of a bus is an event, as it is also for two old ladies sitting in a café in Pinter's play *Black and White* (1959). Yet although the audience must *sense* the characters' boredom, they themselves must not be bored. This is a problem for you to tackle as you examine the play more closely.

Similarly, you will need to confront the problem of continuing relevance. In the workshop activities at the conclusion of this chapter you will find an extract from Wesker's *Chips with Everything* (1962) that is a good example of this problem. The play is about men doing their National Service in Britain in the 1940s and 1950s. To this extent the play is no longer of immediate relevance as nobody is forced to join the Armed Services for a two-year period in Britain now. All the carefully shown details might be thought to be of merely historical interest; but beneath the surface reality of events and conditions there is the whole question of human nature into which Wesker delves, and the military mind is by no means extinct. We might therefore feel that the play has ceased to be a protest against a specific set of conditions and has become more universal in its application. When you study a play you must be careful not to judge its meaning and value solely in relation to a set of social conditions that operated when it was written, although you should certainly be aware of these conditions. Plays of so-called 'social realism' often raise much wider issues and this guarantees them what Dr Jonathan Miller has very aptly described as an 'afterlife'.

Very often you will end up asking yourself 'How real is real?' and that is a very good question to ask. The playwright simulates just as much reality as suits the purpose; indeed, you should now realise that any relation between what happens on a stage and the real world that is being represented all depends on the way in which an audience's perception is being manipulated. Once you get the general feeling from your reading of the play and from your examination of the conventions that it could be described in some senses as 'realistic', take a careful look again at the following features:

- Structure
- Setting
- Situation
- Dialogue

Structure is how a play is put together. Quickly look to see how many Acts, Scenes or episodes the play is divided into and how they are *related*. You may find modern plays that seem like well-made plays, or by contrast a whole series of short episodes that are more like the rapidly changing shots of a film. They may follow sequentially in time or may appear to flash back and forward; they may all take place in one or two or a few places or range over many different locations. You should have detected much of this structure in your examination of the conventions but what now concerns you is how the writer reinforces the sense of reality through the structure of the play. It may be that a series of loosely connected scenes provides a feeling of real life by enabling the audience to build up a complete picture in their imaginations; on the other hand, the sense of truth to real life may be achieved by a deliberate avoidance of climaxes to scenes or of a neat pattern of beginning, middle and end – rather as if the dramatist has taken a random 'slice of life'.

Setting. Look at the details of the setting and the way that the playwright creates the illusion of reality. You may find exhaustive descriptions of rooms, furniture and exteriors and there may be indications of the ways in which the playwright wants the scene to be built on stage. Think of the instructions given at the opening of *The Glass Menagerie*: they involve some contrivance on the part of the scene designer; however, within each space there is careful realism. The majority of modern plays are set indoors and you should pay particular attention to the environment that people create for themselves and which affects them. A junk-filled room, a kitchen or a comfortable lounge, for example, makes a statement that you must interpret. Notice how the playwright builds the environment if the play is set outdoors and look at the stage directions of Strindberg's play *Miss Julie* (1888) that offers a very early example of an intensely realistic setting.

Situation. If you feel that what the playwright presents is in some ways a 'real' situation, try to define and summarise what you mean. You will probably be talking about something that has familiar aspects and that you can explain in logical terms. You are likely also to be able to say why the people are where they are, why they behave as they do and what the consequences of their actions will be. If you are able to imagine that you are witnessing the goings-on in someone else's life, then you will know that a kind of reality has been achieved. Why, you must ask yourself, is this of *interest* to you? Many modern plays show characters trapped by their situation. These characters are usually ordinary people with whom we can identify, and the dramatic interest lies in their response to their predicament.

Dialogue. You will have considered the language of the play in some detail by this time, but think again how this relates to the idea that these are real people talking. Much of the language of well-made plays in the first half of the twentieth century was elegant and witty but represented the real conversation of a small minority of the population. More recent plays, however, have sought to utilise the language patterns of much larger sections of the population, but this is never a static affair: regional characteristics, racial differences, 'imported' vocabulary and new jargon constantly change what we would recognise as 'real' language, so you must look carefully at the play to see how the playwright has created speech patterns that seem up-to-date and yet will not necessarily seem out-dated in a few years. You will find expressions and phrases that relate quite definitely to a certain period of time – identify these and notice how they give authenticity to the action.

▶ The theatre of the absurd

Imagine that you are asked to read Pinter's short play *The Dumb Waiter* (1957). Two men, Ben and Gus, each sit on a bed in a dingy room. One of the men reads out extracts from a newspaper; the other takes off his shoe and discovers that it contains a cigarette packet. They talk in a desultory fashion, debating at some length whether you should say 'light the gas', 'put on the kettle' or 'light the kettle'. They reveal that they are hired assassins. They are in the basement of a restaurant in Birmingham and we know they are waiting for orders about their next 'job'. Thus far, Pinter lulls his audience into a false sense of security about the kind of play this is. Only when the 'dumb waiter' begins to send down absurd messages, crashing down into the room from a supposedly empty upstairs, does the existential dread of the unknown threat begin to seep into the play and into the consciousness of the audience. The familiar has become strange and menacing. In some senses the conversation of the two men seems real, yet it gets nowhere; the characters also seem real, yet we know no more about them at the end of the play than we did at the beginning. In short, we cannot *explain* the play and it presents a view of life that seems chaotic and meaningless.

Such a description would fit all the plays of Samuel Beckett, one of the most influential of all modern dramatists, and, to a lesser extent, those of Eugene Ionesco and Harold Pinter. Other playwrights following their lead included N. F. Simpson, Edward Albee and David Campton. The phenomenon of the so-called 'theatre of the absurd', that had its origins in the 1950s, presents particular difficulties for students because the plays are both inaccessible on the page and frequently baffling on the stage. There are times when reading some plays can be almost as satisfying as reading a good novel, but this is certainly not true of 'absurd' drama. The first thing to grasp is that such plays work by presenting a series of images in the theatre. They are conceived as something that the audience must experience even though they may not be able to offer a logical explanation of the details of that experience. Beckett, for example, offers us images of human beings in varying states of decay: characters in dustbins; characters almost buried in earth; a character in perpetual dialogue with a tape recorder; the mouth of an actress, suspended in darkness and spotlit; a stage cluttered with rubbish, and so on. Time scales are various, with one play, *Breath*, just thirty seconds long; sounds and silence are organised without reference to the normal patterns of everyday life. With his brief theatre pieces Beckett constructed a theatrical image of how we come and go on this earth, briefly filling a void with our bodies and voices, and then disappear into darkness. In order to appreciate these powerful theatrical images you must see and hear them. So, if you cannot get to see a performance of any play you are studying, either organise your own workshop performance yourself or, as a poor substitute, try to imagine it vividly in performance. Picture what the actors actually *do* and how they say the words.

Secondly, you must be honest about what baffles or disturbs you in the play. You will be nearer to appreciating it than you think, because such reactions are probably just what the playwright intended. We shall be looking further at the idea of 'reading' a performance in the next chapter, but at this point don't expect explanations from the play – there won't be any, except that you will begin to get the feeling of what the play is about in a broader sense. You may, for example, never be able to explain why, in what is supposedly a disused restaurant, a dumb waiter suddenly descends bringing messages from outside; yet, as a powerful image of an obscure menace that threatens us from outside and that may be a different fear for every one of us, the dumb waiter is potent and appropriate. On studying the play you may well understand the aptness of David Campton's phrase 'comedy of menace'. You will find the language unnerving if it seems to get nowhere, but again, be honest with your appraisal of it; observe its patterns and clichés and you will find an uncanny resemblance to real speech – indeed, you may find a greater reality in its seemingly disorganised and pointless qualities. Don't allow your expectations that a play should tell a story or 'make sense' to stand in the way of your attitudes and critical analysis.

Thirdly, consider all the ways in which the play frustrates your expectations. The chances are that there will be elements of realism: the setting may be detailed and domestic and the talk may be like ordinary conversation – so you may think, 'Ah, we have a realistic play that will pose a problem that will eventually be resolved', only to be utterly frustrated. Or there may be bizarre elements that prevent you from making any sense of what you see.

In two of Ionesco's plays, for example, the whole stage fills with furniture until, in one of these plays, the two characters on stage have conversations with people whom they imagine to be sitting in the dozens of chairs, whereas in the other play, the actors vanish beneath the furniture. In a further section of this chapter I shall be introducing you to the idea of 'physical theatre' that will have a good number of absurdist elements in this respect. Normally we expect stage furniture to signify that we are looking at a domestic situation and we even deduce information about the status and wealth of the characters from the environment that they have created for themselves. But in Ionesco's plays, furniture seems to serve a different purpose and such deductions become impossible. You may even be equally frustrated by a lack of plot, structure or information about the characters. If you find yourself thinking, 'This is not how a play should be', then you are revealing that you have certain fixed expectations about plays and theatre. You may well share these with many other theatregoers, and the playwright has calculatingly played upon this fact. Notice how the dramatist has worked on traditional theatre forms and reversed some of the processes.

Finally, consider the kind of reality that the playwright *has created*. He or she presents a view of the world through a series of images that may remain imprecise. Reflect on the absurdity of some aspects of our lives and consider how the playwright has conveyed this sense of order.

What does it all mean?
Students often make the mistake of thinking that the meaning of a play is there, embedded in the text, simply waiting for them to dig it out. We shall return to this idea again. Both Beckett and Pinter have always been quite adamant that they are under no obligation to come on at the end of a play and explain the meaning; meanings are created in the minds of the audience both during and after a performance – the text only becomes a play when the audience gives meaning to what they see and hear. Indeed, 'What does this play mean?' is really the wrong question to ask. When asked what his plays were *about*, Harold Pinter once replied, 'The weasel under the cocktail cabinet'. That is a striking metaphor for the fears, guilt, aggression, insecurity and fantasies that operate beneath the surface of our lives and are so vividly portrayed in his plays. Some years after making that remark, Pinter said in a lecture that he felt it had been a great mistake and attempted to clarify his position further by saying 'I can sum up none of my plays. I can describe none of them, except to say: That is what happened. That is what they said. That is what they did.'

Unfortunately, students are expected to be rather more forthcoming than this, but the remark serves as a useful warning to our expectations.

▶ Epic and political theatre

Along with Beckett, the German playwright and director Bertolt Brecht has been one of the strongest influences on the modern theatre. The problem with Brecht is that students study not only his plays but also his various, much publicised, theories about drama, and then find it difficult to relate the two. Because Brecht was both playwright and director, many of his plays evolved during rehearsal and this process has strongly affected the workshop approach that I have adopted in sections of this book. Naturally, Brecht had deep convictions about the way his plays should be performed, but he also had similarly profound beliefs about the theatre in general. All of these opinions have been preserved in his many writings. Students often, quite understandably, forget that Brecht wrote as a result of his wide experience, and that he was not prescribing so much as arguing and reflecting; so, although he may have advocated certain styles of performance and certain aims, this may not be immediately apparent from reading his plays. For example, I have known students to be very worried and to feel inadequate because they couldn't honestly say that they could detect Brecht's famous 'alienation' effect in a play they were reading.

Before you begin looking for Brechtian characteristics in a play you are studying, it might help you to know precisely why Brecht's plays had such an impact in the English-speaking theatre. Brecht's work was first seen in Britain in the 1950s, when the Berliner Ensemble, Brecht's own company, brought their production of *Mother Courage* to London. The idea of an acting 'ensemble' was itself revolutionary; it was a group of actors who regularly worked together, devising the plays with the playwright and rehearsing in an experimental fashion. Such an approach is very common today but in the 1950s it came as a shock that there were no 'stars' and that the democratic group had become committed to a particularly economic style. There was no attempt to deceive the audience into believing that they were not in a theatre: there was no curtain to rise revealing a realistic interior; spotlights were unmasked, and no effort was made to conceal scene changes. The actors, using detailed and realistic props, behaved as if they were telling a story, at one level deeply involved, at another able to stand back from the story and comment upon it. The play itself was a series of short scenes introduced by a projected headline saying what it was about. The setting was the Thirty Years War in Europe, and although there was no plot as such, the events portrayed centred on things that happened to Mother Courage, an anti-heroine who hauled a canteen wagon, trading with rival armies and scheming her way to survival by even allowing her children to die. The action was punctuated by songs in the style of Berliner café songs, and the total effect was to show ordinary fallible people caught up in a futile war with no control over events and confronted by difficult choices.

What I have tried to describe is a piece of what has come to be known as 'Epic Theatre'. This term was invented by an earlier director, Piscator, but it was Brecht who made it famous. The word derives from the German expression to mean 'in episodes' and should not be confused with the word Epic that we use to describe a huge drama. You will also have recognised in my description some techniques of acting and production that Brecht described as the 'alienation' effect. Brecht expected his actors to present a case rather than identify emotionally with the characters they were portraying. In order to 'alienate' the audience, Brecht would also punctuate the realistic action with songs and projected slides. All of this will be familiar to you if you visit the theatre regularly. Brecht developed this style in order that audiences should not become so involved in the story-line and lives of the characters that they were unable to reflect on the issues with which the play was concerned. He constantly insisted that he wanted his audience to be more like the spectators at a sporting event – enjoying the skill of the participants and the contest itself but also able to argue about the outcome. He wanted to confront the audience with a problem and challenge them to think of a solution: to think, not just to feel. Because he wanted plays to serve this didactic purpose, he often called them 'parables' or 'teaching pieces', and because he was a Marxist he insisted that change is possible if people set their minds to it.

Brecht's anti-heroes are often confronted with difficult choices, so the protagonist's predicament is relatively easy to define, but students are often over-serious in their approach to the plays; the plays do deal with very serious issues but you should get a sense of their rich entertainment value too.

A number of fine playwrights with strong political convictions have followed Brecht's lead. John Arden, for example, wrote a play called *Live Like Pigs* (1958) that was interspersed with earthy ballads. David Edgar, Howard Brenton and Howard Barker all came into prominence in the 1970s with plays that presented a socialist viewpoint in a setting that was so colourful, violent and multifarious that they appeared to emulate the style of drama written during the Jacobean era and were accordingly known as the 'New Jacobeans'. During the 1980s the overtly socialist political theatre I have described began to give way to the more personal politics of sexuality, ethnicity and environmentalism. The new, alternative theatre attempted to democratise the division of labour in the theatre itself by developing flexible and collaborative work methods, by introducing theatre to new audiences and by investigating the experiences and interests of groups of oppressed and exploited people whose lives, emotions and aspirations had not been adequately represented in the mainstream theatre. Plays such as *Coming Clean* (1984) by Kevin Elyot, with its explicit scenes of gay sex, or Patrick Marber's *Closer* (1997), exploring ways in which we exploit each other sexually, are examples of plays from these initiatives. Forms of political commitment are represented in the work of companies such as Gay Sweatshop and the feminist company, Monstrous Regiment.

Like Brecht many of the new political playwrights based their plays on actual historical events: Steve Gooch on the Peasants' Revolt in *Will Wat, if not What Will?* (1972), David Hare on the Chinese Revolution in *Fanshen* (1976) and Caryl Churchill on Cromwellian England in *Light Shining in Buckinghamshire* (1977). Such plays inevitably show working people struggling against repressive or exploitative regimes, whereas in plays like John McGrath's *The Cheviot, the Stag and the Black, Black Oil* (1973), Churchill's *Fen* and Steve Wilmer's *Baby Killer* (1981) we see the struggle of ordinary people against the power of huge corporations. Much of the political drama of the last twenty-five years or so has been a response to the attitudes of 'Thatcherism' and 'Reaganomics', but it has also been influenced by the ideas of Artaud. His concept of a 'theatre of cruelty', in which the audience was subjected to an assault on their sensitivities, very often in unconventional theatrical environments, has shaped the way in which many committed small touring theatre companies have presented their work in a variety of unusual settings ranging from factory canteens to the street. Most of the work of this kind has made use of the structures and techniques popularised by Brecht, and when you come to study these plays I would suggest that, having used the additional steps I suggested for 'realistic' plays, you look at the Brechtian plays under the following headings:

- Structure
- Staging
- Situation

Structure. Examine the choice of episodes. They will not usually be causally related, so discover in what sense they *are* related. Note the total time scale of the play and any linking device, such as story-teller, narrator or headlines. Pay particular attention to the positioning of the songs – don't skip over these but try to hear an original musical setting of them. Decide on the effect that a song directed straight at the audience will have. How does a song in a Brechtian play differ from a song in a romantic 'musical'?

Staging. Plays by Brecht and those who have used some of his techniques often appear to demand elaborate scenery, but in fact are designed to be staged with great economy. Look very carefully at the stage conventions.

Notice how locations – interiors, exteriors and combinations of these – can be represented simply, often by no more than a central property such as a table, cart or bar on an otherwise bare stage. Such properties, along with film and slide projections and on-stage musicians, play a vital part in transforming the stage space so that it represents something concrete in the minds of the audience. Think how different this approach is from the realism of Ibsen or Strindberg, where the room itself almost seems to be a character in the play. If you think through this difference you will see how it extends to the performance style. In the play of any realistic playwright it would be unacceptable for an actor to step out of role in the carefully constructed room and talk to the audience, but in a piece of epic theatre there is a two-way traffic between stage and auditorium – rather like the relationship between a stand-up comic and his or her audience. British and American audiences have never quite responded to Brecht's plays in the way that, for example, East Europeans have done. In these countries it is still possible to find theatres packed with people of all types and generations laughing and applauding at his plays. In the English-speaking world, the problem is partly that it is only recently that we have had workable translations of what are often wonderfully poetic and witty plays. We have also allowed productions of Brecht to be approached with a deep seriousness that suffocates them.

Situation. Epic theatre poses social and moral problems for the audience to consider. Once you have identified the dilemmas facing the hero or anti-hero, decide what social or moral issues these raise. You might remember that the American philosopher and writer George Santayana once said 'Life is not a spectacle or a feast; it is a predicament.' Often a character is faced with a difficult choice, so you must consider the basis for condemning or approving any choice that the character makes and try to understand the consequences. You also need to have a very clear idea of the pressures that a particular situation creates. Even if the play deals with events that are far removed from us both in time and place, you must determine what gives them relevance to a modern audience.

▶ Expressionism

In the play *The Emperor Jones* (1925) by the American playwright Eugene O'Neill, we see a fictional state ruled over by a dictatorial former criminal who has proclaimed himself as Emperor. Neither the action nor the dialogue in this play could comfortably be described as realistic and the total effect of seeing this play or even of reading it for the first time is rather like watching a cartoon. However, there is no doubting the *inner* reality of the ideas and subject of the play, even if the *external* reality seems distorted. Such a play is described as Expressionist.

It can become tiresome in the study of modern drama if your whole time is taken up by understanding a number of 'isms', but it is important to recognise some of the characteristics of significant movements in the modern theatre so that you can at least be aware of certain trends and be able to discuss them. Expressionism as a term was introduced into the Arts in the very early years of the twentieth century in France, although most people would now consider the most obviously Expressionist painting to be *The Scream* by Edvard Munch. Some critics would argue that the first true expressionist play was *Woyzeck* written by the German Georg Buchner in 1836. This unfinished play, in which the scenes are often tiny fragments that could be performed in a number of different orders, established the form of plays with terse dialogue, episodic structure and grotesque characterisation that was later developed by Strindberg in his play *To Damascus* (1898–1901).

From about 1910 to 1924, particularly in Germany, Expressionism gave rise to a large body of plays that often required almost dream-like physical settings to enhance their serious and often violent scenes. Such settings could be achieved through the developing techniques of stage lighting and recorded sound. The language, too, often had soaring, verse-like qualities that sought to express complex ideas and emotions for which ordinary prose seemed inadequate. Although this episode in modern drama is a relatively brief one, Expressionism did influence a significant number of Irish and American playwrights and we can see this in the plays of W. B. Yeats, O'Casey and O'Neill.

Some of the ideas of the expressionist theatre have permeated what we now refer to as 'Physical Theatre' and we must briefly consider this newer movement in modern drama so that you have a wide range of styles that you can recognise and discuss.

▶ Late modernism and postmodernism

In the opening chapter of this book I pointed out that one of the characteristics of modern drama was that it explored the human condition in an age of science and technology. As the twentieth century progressed, this relationship grew ever more complex. On the one hand, there had been remarkable advances in communications, medicine and engineering that radically improved the material quality of life, and, on the other hand, the development of increasingly hideous weapons and the appearance of terrifying diseases: AIDS, various forms of cancer, BSE and Foot & Mouth that science seemed impotent to control. This dichotomy, which raises many serious and ethical issues, has produced a profound sense of unease in the modern world that has been reflected in plays and performances. For example, we have a large number of plays on the subject of war: R. C. Sherriff's *Journey's End* (1928) and McGuinness's *Observe the Sons of Ulster Marching Towards the Somme* (1985) show the mechanical fury and waste of the First World War; *The Long and the Short and the Tall* (1958), by Willis Hall, explores the brutality of the Second World War; and Tony Marchant's *Welcome Home* (1983) gives a disturbing account of the Falklands War. The threat of nuclear annihilation is dealt with in Ann Jellicoe's *The Rising Generation* (1960) and David Campton's *Then* (1958).

Playwrights have also confronted the threat of disease in their writing: Larry Kramer's *The Normal Heart* (1988) was the first of several plays to deal with AIDS, and both Louise Page in *Tissue* (1978) and Josie Melia in *Beestings* (1999) consider the impact of breast cancer. Judy Upton wrestles with the issues raised by the prospect of organ transplants from pigs in *Pig in the Middle* (2000).

Perhaps one of the most disturbing plays of the twentieth century is Tony Kushner's two-part, seven-hour play *Angels in America* (1992). Here he presents a picture of lurking fascism in US politics, the effects of the demise of Communism, the rise of fundamentalism in religion, the spread of AIDS, the poison of racism, and faith, God and angels.

Many of the plays and production modes we have just been considering exhibit the characteristics of a philosophical and critical approach known as 'postmodernism' that emerged during the second half of the twentieth century and has continued into the twenty-first. Postmodernism challenges the whole idea that objective truth can be established through rational, scientific thought and that human beings can consciously take control of their destiny. For the postmodernist there are no absolute values, no meanings beyond those constructed by individuals as a result of experience and no 'grand design' (or meta narrative) outside life as we know it. In the postmodern world the highest goal is self-expression; institutions are seen as instruments of control; language regarded with suspicion because its meanings rely on usage in a social context and people are likely to manipulate each other. Postmodernist society is characterised by fragmentation, cynicism and distrust; there is an underlying pessimism about personal freedom and, because only human beings create values, objectivity and objective judgements become almost impossible.

It is difficult to place a precise date on the beginning of the 'postmodern' age but the contemporary sociologist Jean Baudrillard suggests that 'early modernity' is the period between the Renaissance and the Industrial Revolution, 'modernity' is the period at the start of the Industrial Revolution and 'postmodernity' is the period of the mass media. From this we can see that the periods covered by this book encompass these significant shifts in attitude.

The titles of two plays seem to typify the postmodern world: *A Mad World, My Masters* (1977) by Barrie Keeffe and *Shopping and Fucking* (1996) by Mark Ravenhill. Keeffe's play is a modern reworking of a Jacobean play by Thomas Middleton of the same name and is a farce full of black comedy in which the manipulative nature of the 'upper class' in British society is explored. A similar theme dominates Peter Barnes's black political farce *The Ruling Class* (1969). It can be argued that the 'farce' is the ultimate post-modernist genre, because even though the characters find themselves in absurd situations they are forced to give explanations knowing that there is no absolute truth. For example, in the opening scene of *The Ruling Class* the 13th Earl of Gurney hangs himself in his library wearing a three-cornered hat, a ballet skirt, long underwear and a sword. His dying speech in no way explains or justifies the act and the audience is left to construct a meaning out of logical chaos.

The use of black comedy is particularly evident in the work of Joe Orton. *Entertaining Mr. Sloane* (1964) provoked a very hostile reception because of its treatment of sexuality; but the play shows a world in which there are no fixed moral absolutes and the characters can only claim that their individual form of sexuality is 'right'. In *What the Butler Saw* (1967), a farce revolving around psychiatry and the disappearance of the cigar from a statue of Winston Churchill, the characters solve nothing by discovering the 'truth': chaos and anarchy seem to be the natural state. In Orton's *Loot* (1966) as in Keeffe's *A Mad World, My Masters* the police are shown as anarchic because they are defending a system based on absolute morality that does not exist. In all these plays there *is* a social order but it is made up of what others impose upon the characters. Therefore, it is not so much the social order that is threatened by the behaviour of the characters, but the characters themselves threatened by the social order.

The title of Mark Ravenhill's play *Shopping and Fucking* suggests that in the postmodern world the only two certainties are sex and consumerism, and, indeed, Patrick Marber shows in the scenes in *Closer*, set in a lap-dancing club, that sex can be a form of consumerism. An even more potent attack on the sex industry is mounted in Anthony Minghella's *Made in Bangkok* (1987). This play shows the ruthless and exploitative nature of this industry and reveals the abuse as a form of violence. Many recent plays are not only anarchic but violent in language, content and performance. In Tony Marchant's *The Attractions* (1988) we see a museum devoted to the instru-ments used for murder, yet one of the characters, Ruth, protests 'there's no care in your conversation. No respect of anyone, anything'; whereas Danny, who has come to make a success of the museum with its ghastly exhibits, remarks, 'That's why it's so popular. We're as savage as they are . . . if you want to be modern, you forget about restraint.' This statement appears to be true of the plays of Sarah Kane whose writing career was tragically cut short by her suicide in 1999. In her play *Blasted*, an abusive sexual relationship between father and daughter is extended into a play of hideous physical action that profoundly shocked audiences and critics at its premiere although they recognised that they were in the presence of a new and original talent.

Many of the nihilistic plays of modern drama are a rejection of the institution of the conventional theatre itself. For example, the 'Underground Theatre', which flourished in Greenwich Village and San Francisco in the 1960s and '70s, frequently featured plays by such writers as Sam Shepard, Jean-Claude van Italie and Murray Mednick that were a direct antithesis of the psychological realism of well-made plays by Ibsen, Miller and O'Neill that seemed to dominate the serious drama on Broadway. As we have seen, a similar process emerged in the 'fringe' and 'alternative' theatres in Britain.

I do not wish to give the impression that any playwright has set out to write a play to be labelled 'postmodernist', but we can see that the ideas and attitudes of a postmodernist world have influenced the kind of plays being written. In a fascinating play, *Travesties* (1974) by Tom Stoppard, there is a debate between Henry Carr and a librarian, Cecily, that is relevant to our response to any challenging play, be it political or dealing with some personal issue. Cecily says 'We live in an age when the social order is seen to be the work of material forces and we have been given an entirely new kind of responsibility, the responsibility of changing society.' Carr, however, responds: 'My dear girl – art doesn't change society, it is merely changed by it.'

Many of the plays I have mentioned in this section provide a bleak but honest view of the world as the playwright sees it. As students, we must recognise not only what the playwright or performance is saying but how it is said. We shall return to this issue when we consider some recent critical approaches to the study of drama and performance.

▶ Physical and improvisatory theatre

I am going to conclude this chapter dealing with different kinds of plays with a brief consideration of an increasingly popular form of theatre that is not derived from a written text. Because the emphasis in much modern drama study is on reading the written text and because we most certainly can derive a great deal from reading that text, we sometimes forget that it is the shaping of that text into a physical form that makes it drama. Words are not essential for drama; many cultures have rich strands of traditional physical theatre that have also influenced the development of English-speaking and Western drama.

In what is now understood by physical theatre, it is not the words that predominate, but the totality of the performance of the actors who are now required to work with a range and dexterity unknown to some of their predecessors. Beckett's own production of his play *Waiting for Godot* was more like a ballet than a conventional play. Bodies moving in space were important for his concept of drama.

Perhaps the most impressive piece of physical theatre seen in Britain was Theatre de Complicite's production of *The Street of Crocodiles* (1992), based on the stories of the Polish writer Bruno Schultz. This innovative company was founded in 1986 as a collective, and has combined movement, text and design in order to achieve the maximum expression of meaning. Other companies have followed their example and now insist that actors may have to possess acrobatic, juggling and other circus skills, be able to play musical instruments, sing, work with mime and masks or dance or manipulate trick scenery. They may be surrounded by all manner of sounds and music; they may inhabit an environment of planks, ladders, scaffolding, items that collapse on impact or ropes and swings; they may use everyday objects in the most unexpected ways. Some of the most challenging ideas in physical theatre come from the world of contemporary dance: the works of Pina Bausch, for example, are as much part of modern theatre as are the plays of Tony Kushner.

In a recent production by a group named 'Stretch People', two actors, using very sophisticated balancing and mime techniques, created a complete scenario of the 'lives' of several upright vacuum cleaners – including the birth of a baby cleaner from the bag of a mother. The entire theatre was held spellbound as one actor, accompanying himself on the guitar, sang a lullaby to the new arrival.

Physical theatre involves a good deal of improvisation on the part of the actors, but there is also a form of drama that develops texted material from improvisation. This technique has been used most effectively by the British playwright Mike Leigh, who is now probably better known for his work in film where he adopts similar approaches. Leigh provides his actors with some initial starting points but demands that they develop characters and situations through research, improvisation and discussion. The final product will be a scripted piece of work of great intensity, and some of his plays have become established classics in the modern theatre. For students studying drama, physical and improvisational theatre pose something of a problem if they rely exclusively on reading written texts. Making sense of all forms of theatre will be the subject of my next chapter.

Checklist

Key topics covered in this chapter:

- Tackling a wide range of plays
- Realism and Naturalism
- The well-made play
- Definitions of: a thesis or problem play, theatre of the absurd and epic theatre
- Understanding Expressionism
- The influence of Brecht on political theatre
- Late Modernism and Postmodernism
- Physical Theatre and Improvisatory Theatre

▶ Workshop activities

1. Printed below is an extract from Arnold Wesker's play *Chips with Everything*. Once you have read the extract, work on it with a small group and discuss the various steps I have suggested for tackling a play showing a great deal of social realism. Then improvise further scenes that you might imagine the play to contain or obtain a copy of the play and select four key scenes that show the predicament in which young people undertaking National Service found themselves.

    Here is the extract: you need to know that a Meteor was a jet fighter plane used by the RAF at the time this play was written.

    Sound of marching feet. Marching stops. The lecture hall.
    Boys enter and sit on seats. Enter the WING COMMANDER, *boys rise.*
    WING COMMANDER. Sit down, please. I'm your Wing Commander. You think we are at peace. Not true. We are never at peace. The human being is in a constant state of war and we must be prepared, each against the other. History has taught us this and we must learn. The reasons why and wherefore are not our concern. We are simply the men who must be prepared. You, why do you look at me like that?
    PIP. I'm paying attention, sir.
    WING COMMANDER. There's insolence in those eyes, lad – I recognise insolence in a man; take that glint out of your eyes, your posh tones don't fool me. We are simply the men who must be prepared. Already the

aggressors have a force far superior to ours. Our efforts must be intensified. We need a fighting force and it is for this reason you are being trained here, according to the best traditions of the RAF. We want you to be proud of your part, unashamed of the uniform you wear. But you must not grumble too much if you find that government facilities for you, personally, are not up to standard. We haven't the money to spare. A Meteor, fully armed, is more important than a library. The CO of this camp is called Group Captain Watson. His task is to check any tendency in his officers to practical jokes, to discountenance any disposition in his officers to gamble or indulge in extravagant expenditure; to endeavour, by example and timely intervention, to promote a good understanding and to prevent disputes. Group Captain Watson is a busy man, you will rarely see him. You, why are you smiling?

SMILER. I'm not sir, it's natural, I was born like it.

WING COMMANDER. Because I want this taken seriously, you know, from all of you. Any questions?

WILFE. Sir, if the aggressors are better off than us, what are they waiting for?

WING COMMANDER. What's your name?

WILFE. 247 Seaford, sir.

WING COMMANDER. Any other questions?

Exit. Enter SQUADRON LEADER. The boys rise.

(*New English Dramatists 7*, Penguin, 1965, pp. 25–6)

2. Select an incident from the history of your locality for which substantial documentation and records exist. Devise a short 'Documentary Drama' using as many Brechtian techniques as possible to relate the incident.

3. Select a scene from any play with which you are familiar and present it in a number of contrasting styles; using the various types of play considered in this chapter as models.

8 Making a Critical Response

Students are often concerned if they feel that *they* cannot find in a play all that teachers, critics and other students claim to have noticed. You may have felt this as you followed some of the suggestions in this book, but you must remember not to expect everything to come to you at once. The more you acquaint yourself with a play by reading, workshop activities or theatre visits, the more you need to *think* about the play for ideas to settle in your mind. No good play is going to yield up all its qualities immediately; the very fact that it amuses, interests, baffles or angers you should mean that it lingers in the mind, and things will occur to you long after you have closed the book or left the theatre. Sometimes a chance remark or a piece of criticism will illuminate something that puzzled you weeks ago. This, of course, is hardly much comfort in the highly pressurised world of examination-based study, but it is a good reason for distrusting some of your initial responses and for giving yourself time to return to a play after a short lapse. Don't be afraid, either, to change your mind, if after a period of thought, or a visit to the theatre you begin to see things differently. At this point I am going to introduce you to some ideas from modern critical theory that may be of help in bringing together all the aspects of study outlined in this book.

▶ Making use of critical theory

It is obviously necessary for drama students to be able to study certain plays irrespective of whether they can see a performance, and it is equally obvious that for every performance that is given, a host of other, different performances could be imagined. For these reasons students have to deal with printed texts of plays more often than with live performances. It is therefore important, in the first place, to distinguish between what is conveyed by the printed text and what is conveyed by the performance. A printed text consists of only two codes of communication: dialogue (sometimes monologue) and stage directions. The stage directions may be explicit or merely implicit, but they are present in the text of every play at least in the minimal form of *who* is speaking and *where*. The experience of seeing a play performed in a theatre, on the other hand, is a very different experience: a variety of codes of communication present themselves to the spectators simultaneously and all compete for their attention. The settings, the costumes, the music, the lights, the movements as well as the words, all offer to the spectator their peculiar sequence of sign systems. Various elements of the production will rotate to move into the foreground of the spectator's attention, while the rest becomes background. In other words, each separate sign system will be decoded by the spectators with reference to all the others. For example, an actor going through the movements of a sword fight will be understood by the audience quite differently according to whether he does so in the setting of a medieval castle or of a modern padded cell.

In using terms like 'codes of communication', or 'sign system', we are borrowing from a school of criticism usually known as 'Structuralism'. When applied to literature, this method has demolished the traditional idea that a text can function like a transparent screen between the writer and reader. Traditionally the identity of both the reader and writer and of the meaning of a story had been assumed to be fixed, in some sense *there*, waiting to be discovered. The Structuralist critics have shown that the identities of both reader and writer are constructed by and through the process of exchange and communication. We can see that if meaning in literature is constructed rather than found, then the theatre is even more complex, because meaning is constructed both by the performers and the spectators.

These new approaches to literary criticism can help us with the study of drama because they serve to remind us that any approach to the theatre must somehow take account of the variety of different sign systems through which the theatre communicates. The idea of the sign system has been developed by Structuralist critics, especially Roland Barthes, to show that we are perpetually 'reading' messages in the objects that surround us, but they are messages not communicated in words. For example, the tape recorder that we see on stage in *Death of a Salesman* stands for the tape-recorder in Howard Wagner's office. But it stands for much more than that: we can 'read' it as the latest gadget acquired by a consumer society that is rapidly devaluing human life; it is the new object of attention that prevents Howard, the boss, from giving proper attention to his employee Willy Loman. We can read it as a symbol of everything that makes the ruthless materialism of the play so ugly. In Ibsen's plays, the quality of the light has to be 'read' by the audience: sometimes, like truth it is too bright to bear and at other times it is murky, like the characters' motives.

The ideas of postmodernism have provided a number of new ways of thinking critically about drama. For postmodernist critics the emphasis is on performance, because it is only at that point that meanings can be constructed. As we have seen, in their terminology the play is 'the work' whereas the 'text' is the course of the action of which words are only one part. Very often it is pointed out that the text of one work will contain elements of or references to another text. There are good examples of this 'inter-textuality' in the play *Crave* (1998) by Sarah Kane, in which sections of the dialogue by the characters named C, M, B and A contain frequent biblical references, and in Joe Orton's *What the Butler Saw*, which has many references and structural similarities to Oscar Wilde's *The Importance of Being Earnest* (1895). In the postmodern way of thinking about performance, intertext is often related to popular culture: you may remember that *Teendreams* by David Edgar draws heavily on pop music to establish time and ethos. For postmodernists, of course, there is no hierarchy of art forms or modalities, and popular culture, be it graffiti or the latest dance craze, is as deserving of serious consideration as any other 'work'.

Another postmodernist view is that when a work has been created the author abdicates all rights of ownership once it is in performance. This attitude leads to some extraordinary and frequently controversial interpretations of plays. Both Arthur Miller and Samuel Beckett have been involved in heated disputes and lawsuits over productions of their plays that they considered illegitimate. The emphasis on performance as a subject of study has, in fact, led to the emergence of the new discipline of 'Performance Studies'. This has reflected the increasing tendency to integrate art forms such as drama, dance, music or circus skills that had previously been studied separately. For students studying modern drama these developments provide a useful vocabulary and way of thinking about what they read, see and take part in. Instead of responding to new performances with anger and bafflement, as many contemporary newspaper critics do, we can analyse what is happening and form fresh views on the relationship between the original work and the performed text. In your workshop activities you will create a text every time you work on the suggested material. This text may be a personal narrative with or without words or a deliberate reference to another text that may or not be a play. You will then be in a good position to observe and reflect upon this process when you read a play or attend a performance.

With all these thoughts in mind I'm going to help you to bring together all your insights so that we can explore an imaginary theatre visit. This should give you confidence in making your own critical response.

▶ Organising your ideas

A visit to any theatre production, however 'good' or 'bad', can be very useful, and for this reason I am going to imagine that you are visiting a professional production of Pinter's play *The Birthday Party*, which you have been required to study. I shall guide you through the first few minutes, showing you how you might observe and analyse many key features of the play.

The first thing you notice when you take your seat is that the stage is an open, thrust stage that projects into the auditorium and that there are no curtains. As you look around you see the various spotlights hung ready to light the stage and you may reflect on the influence that Brecht has had on modern theatre – there is no attempt to disguise the fact that you *are* in a theatre. Positioned in the centre of the stage area is the set – there is a rather dingy room furnished with solid but drab furniture and decorated with fading wallpaper and tasteless ornaments. A staircase leads into the room on one side, above it there is an archway of moulded plaster and beside it the door over which there is a glass panel with a house name on it that you can see written back-to-front because it is intended to be read from outside. On the other side of the room is another door and a serving hatch, both of which lead to a kitchen in which there is a real kitchen sink. You may not have thought of this play as a 'kitchen sink' drama, but there is the sink. All this detail is actually conveyed by one long wall that runs at a slight angle across the rear of the stage and two very short walls that are attached at either end and project forwards towards the auditorium. These two short walls are actually cut away as though someone has taken a pair of scissors and randomly trimmed them, and the edges seem to fade into the black background of the stage. The 'floor' area is designated by a carpet, but even this is cut off, because its front edge merges into the front edge of the stage; and although a single light bulb hangs in the middle of the 'room' there is actually no ceiling and the upper boundaries merge into darkness.

How easily you accept all of this highly artificial contrivance as 'realistic'! There are enough real and familiar objects for this setting to represent a room in a run-down boarding house and, although some of the details may differ from what you were expecting, the characters who you know will walk through the door will fit perfectly into this environment created by the stage designer, and all the events of the play will 'work' in this setting. There is the packet of cornflakes, the breakfast table, the tatty mixture of chairs and so on. You can 'read' all this as signifying the play you have examined.

The sense of reality created leads you to believe that the play will provide clear explanations, for, as the philosopher A. H. Ryan puts it, 'what we look for is that information which, when appropriately put together, yields us an argument to the effect that the event in question was what we should rationally expect'. You know that this idea, which will dominate the attitude of the audience, will, in the case of this play, be upset and frustrated. Rational explanations are likely to be lacking, but, whereas a play with surrealist scenery might lead us to expect them to be missing, the recognisable interior with its staircase and kitchen makes the audience think otherwise.

All this is available for you to observe before the play begins, and it is important that you take the trouble to do so. You are already thinking about the decisions that are being made, reflecting on the degree of realism, and on the conventions adopted by the playwright and director, and are starting to 'read' the performance. You *could* waste your time at this point, but once the action starts you won't get so good a chance to think constructively about some of these issues.

When the house light dims there is a brief total darkness before the stage lights come up to reveal Meg, the landlady, already in her kitchen banging about with crockery and saucepans and turning on the tap to fill a kettle. Again, you accept without question that the rooms *are* lit by the light bulbs that you see hanging and which are turned on by the brass switch you see by the door. But, *in fact*, a couple of dozen spotlights are focused on the stage area. As Meg, a woman in her late fifties you think, continues with what seem like breakfast preparations, her husband Petey enters. He wears a brown overall, a peaked cap and a ticket machine. You know he is a deckchair attendant if you have read the play; if you haven't, that fact, and the fact that Petey and Meg are married, are established through the dialogue quite early on. Petey slowly removes his cap, overall and ticket machine, hangs them up, takes a cardigan, puts it on, sits at the table, opens the newspaper and begins to eat his cornflakes. Meg calls out, 'Is that you?' and there follows a desultory conversation through the serving hatch about cornflakes and fried bread. A little later they talk about the contents of the newspaper – you observe the simple, repetitive patterns of their dialogue that look so flat on the page but that now sound so real, so inconsequential and so funny. In spite of the fact that there are no jokes, no comic business and no obviously farcical situations, the audience are laughing almost from the first word spoken. You notice, also, the long and quite frequent silences, the fact that no 'story' as such appears to be unfolding in the dialogue, and the extra-ordinary sense that these two people are going through a ritual in which they consciously avoid real communication. At one level it seems meaningless, yet it does establish a cosy social order: this feeling of social order is enhanced by the references to Stanley, who is not yet up and therefore not on the stage – a pattern that Pinter exploits to the full in the dialogue. You notice, therefore, when this social order is threatened: when Petey mentions that two men came up to him on the beach and enquired about staying at the boarding house, the simple scene of *exposition*, which gives some indication of what the general situation is, moves into the first phase of *complication*. You sense this in the theatre through the tension that the mention of the two men produces in Meg and, later, in Stanley, the only guest currently staying with her. You will also be aware how the conversations among the five characters in the play have their own distinctive rhythms depending on who is present.

None of this observation prevents you from enjoying the performance or being affected by it. You will be aware of the effect that the performance is having on the audience. As each character enters you will quickly readjust your mental picture of him or her to accord with the new image of the character presented by the actor or actress. Meg may look younger than you had expected, Stanley older; Lulu may be a cockney although you had imagined her coming from Birmingham. As you watch the play you are struck by how little the characters reveal about themselves. When Stanley, who has once supposedly been a pianist on the pier, gives an account of a concert he gave in Lower Edmonton, you begin to doubt the truth of it and you realise that the text of the play appears to be almost like the sub-text. The most disturbing things to witness are the games that the characters play – at first apparently harmless, as with the games between Meg and Stanley, but then increasingly sinister and deadly. Suddenly watching a game or a ritual is totally different from imagining it, and the moments when the characters and the audience are plunged into darkness are chilling.

Your experience in the theatre is a mixture of analysis and emotional involvement. You now have a chance to see the practical implications of what you have studied in private. I have described here a production that I actually was involved with myself and I realise that it may have been very different from a production of the same play that you have seen. But what precise codes of communication were involved as I offered this description of an imaginary theatre visit? I would suggest the following:

- The linguistic. That is, the words that appeared in any shape or form.
- The perceptual. That is, anything that makes a direct impact on the senses of the audience and all those elements that have significance not filtered through language.
- The socio-cultural. This is the significance that will be attached to elements of the linguistic or the perceptual according to the conventions of a particular society or culture (e.g. British audiences recognise the world of the seaside boarding house).
- The theatrical. These are theatrical conventions, or to use the language of structuralism, 'codes of signification'.

You will see that these categories do help you to organise your thoughts and provide a way of analysing and describing a live performance.

What I have said should also enable you to bring together many of the strands of this book. You see the protagonist struggling with the predicament, you see the effect on people of the breakdown of social order, and your ear detects the features of dialogue you have studied. There is enormous pleasure in hearing what you have identified as the key speeches performed, and you may feel that you need to rethink aspects of their meaning – notice the concrete decisions made about inflections, emphasis or pause in speeches you know well; another 'reading' adds to your fund of experience and terms of reference. Notice, also, how the designer has interpreted or adapted the scenic requirements, how the director has located the action in a precise historical period, and how the audience react to what they see. For a serious student of drama all this is more important than whether you thought the performance was 'good', because you should now have far wider terms of reference than such a comment implies – any live performance can reinforce your study of the play and give you a far clearer idea of what you mean when you come to write about it in a review, an essay or examination question. It is to these tasks that I shall turn in the next chapter.

Checklist

Key topics covered in this chapter:

- Using some of the ideas of Structuralism to help in your play analysis
- Performance Studies
- What it means to 'read' a performance
- Gaining the maximum possible benefit from a theatre visit
- Organising your response to a live performance
- Bringing together all the strands of this book to enable you to respond to a written and performed text

9 Exams and Essays

▶ One last push

I hope that by now you have gained a great deal of confidence from the various steps that I have suggested, but of course there is no substitute for knowing your material thoroughly. It is the characters and themes that make a play interesting, and because both these aspects of drama are favourite topics for essays and exam questions, there are a few things I need to emphasise about them before you attempt any written answers.

By the time you have studied a play carefully, you should feel as if you know all the characters personally. You should be able to talk about them as you could about a close friend or relation. The one thing that you will realise about people you know well is that they are very complex, and the same will be true of characters in a play. The playwright offers a view of the world and of the process of being alive; that view will reflect the fact that life is a strangely complicated affair. The more you know someone, and the more you discover about a character, the more you find that that person is full of contradictions, inconsistencies, prejudices, mixed motives, beliefs and other attractive and less attractive features. No simple statement will ever adequately sum up a complete character, although you may well be able to sum up important *aspects* of a character.

When you consider a character you should list those external pressures that make that character act in a particular way. Many of Brecht's plays show characters who act out of a need to survive; they cannot afford the luxury of moral scruples because the choice is between survival and extermination. You may argue that a person should never compromise his or her convictions and should even be prepared to die for them. Thomas Becket chooses this path in *Murder in the Cathedral* and becomes a martyr and tragic hero; Brecht, however, puts the choice to the audience and emphasises all the pressures that capitalist society places upon its members.

You will see that as you build up a set of ideas as to *why* a character acts as he or she does there are many factors to be taken into consideration. In the study of modern drama we have to remember that playwrights and we ourselves are likely to use rational scientific explanations for human behaviour. During the period I have defined as 'modern', the sciences of psychology and sociology have increasingly taken over from religion as a means of accounting for people's individual and group conduct. We now tend to think, for example, that our subconscious mind in some way stores experiences from the past and shapes our present behaviour. Thus many modern plays are concerned with the past and its sometimes ghostly presence in the present. Plays also show an interest in the nature of dreams and in various kinds of neurosis. Similarly, we now tend to describe society in political and economic terms and are very concerned about the effects of class, technology and various forms of government. The erosion of religious belief, the impact of two world wars, many other horrific conflicts and the more recently acquired potential for the human race to obliterate itself have all deeply affected the way in which modern dramatists have portrayed people trying to live in the world. What I am anxious to underline here is that modern drama takes account of all the varying factors that are seen to shape human life, so that when you study a character from a play, you are likely to find them provided with motives, attitudes, behavioural characteristics and situations that can be investigated and largely explained in these terms.

What should also have emerged in your study is an understanding that the problems and predicaments with which the characters become entangled are invariably linked to questions larger than the characters themselves. When Mother Courage in Brecht's play refuses to recognise her own son at the moment of his death, it isn't simply her dilemma that we recognise: it is the whole theme of suffering, survival and expediency. In the same way, when we watch the behaviour of the characters in Shaw's plays *Heartbreak House* (1917) and *Misalliance* (1910), we are seeing a microcosm of Edwardian England, England floundering around in a dream-like state before the First World War and, as in the symbol of the conservatory in *Misalliance*, living in a very fragile peace. Shaw's, like Stoppard's characters, talk a great deal and will often draw attention to the themes they are exploring – problems of class or of the nature of language itself, perhaps. One of the attractions of drama is that it is capable of dealing with very complicated issues, and one of the pleasures of studying a play is to be able to recognise the themes and issues and be able to discuss them.

That is why I have left this to the end. You have been through all the detail now, and, as my tutor used to say to me, you can 'relax and expand'. Students so often fail at this final stage because they are afraid to say, 'Well, I've recognised all the conventions and I've got all this detail, but what really *are* the issues and themes raised by this play?' Some recent examination questions illustrate this: examples I have in front of me suggest that *Waiting for Godot* is 'about the realities of everyday life – half understanding and noncommunicating'; that 'Ethics is a complicated business' is relevant to Stoppard's *Professional Foul*; or that 'To do the right deed for the wrong reason' is a key to the central theme of *Murder in the Cathedral*. Notice how these questions that you are asked to discuss either take a key phrase from the text and ask you to reflect how that gives clues to what the play is really about, or they simply make a statement that you are asked to consider. In either case you need to have reduced your final view of the play to a few strong statements that seem to you to sum up the essence. Once you have done that privately, after a lot of reflection, try comparing your statements with those of critics and with the sort of quotations that you will find on exam papers. Remember, your opinion is as valid as anyone else's provided you can back it up with solid evidence. And that brings us to the whole question of writing essays and tackling examinations.

▶ Planning and writing your answers

Writing an essay in an examination or as part of course work ought to be an enjoyable conclusion to your period of study. Examiners are anxious to share your enthusiasm for drama and, as many of their reports reveal, they are quick to notice if you have gained enjoyment from your work. The questions they set test your ability to enter into and think seriously about the world of the play and there is never any attempt to confuse or mystify you. All written work seeks to evaluate your knowledge *and* understanding. Examiners are human; and their relief and pleasure when they find an answer that genuinely responds to the question and shows that a candidate has engaged with the issues of the play, is considerable.

I am going to assume that the process for writing essays and examination answers is virtually the same, although, obviously, outside the exam situation you have more planning time and can write at greater length. You should remember that your examiners are perfectly aware of this fact, and they are certainly not going to set you an exam question that requires more than about four or five sides to answer. You can also be sure that no question is going to require you to write about every aspect of a play. The logical steps you should go through in responding to any essay title are the same, regardless of the topic, and so the advice I give should cover all your written responses.

Exams in modern drama invariably consist of two main kinds of question. The first kind asks you a direct question about the themes and issues of the play, the characters, or an aspect of the dramatist's technique. There may also be questions of this kind that relate to more than one of these topics. For example,

How successfully does Miller present Willy Loman's increasingly weak grip on his life in *Death of a Salesman*?

This is obviously a question about Miller's technique *and* a character. This does not necessarily make it more difficult. Questions of this kind will also contain a quotation, either from the play itself or from a critic, and you will be asked to discuss this quotation in relation to your understanding of the play. An example of this type of question is:

'Beckett's plays are sad because he is obsessed by human despair, by reflecting on man's inability even to make a decision, much less carry it out.' Discuss this remark in relation to *Waiting for Godot*.

Don't be put off by the *length* of such questions: they are no more difficult than the short ones, such as

Are the characters of *Waiting for Godot* sufficiently differentiated?

which comes from the same examination paper!

All the questions I have discussed so far, particularly those containing a quotation, have the advantage of identifying for you the issues you are to think about. As I have said, no one is going to ask you a question about every aspect of the play, and the *question itself* will define for you the area to which you must limit your answer. This is a very good reason for reading the question extremely carefully instead of doing what many students do: flounder around hoping to hit upon the right topic by chance. I need to say some important things about reading questions, but before I do, I must mention the other main type of question: *an extract from a play on which you are asked to comment in some way*. This kind of question is increasingly popular as a means of allowing students to show what they can derive from reading a piece of dramatic text. Obviously it involves more reading time and may thus lead to shorter answers, but it demands a rather different approach from the first kind of question and I shall deal with it at the end of this chapter. Even at this point, however, I must emphasise that close attention to the text of a play is still regarded as the most important single aspect of an examination.

There are three points for you to remember *whatever* kind of question you are tackling.

1. There are *no preconceived correct answers*. Examiners do not have a series of 'right' and 'wrong' categories, except for facts that you might use to support your argument. Examination questions provide you with

an opportunity to show your understanding and appreciation of what you have been studying, and provided you can back up what you say with evidence from the play, your opinion is valid. Examiners are interested in your personal response to a play, and your job is to show that you've allowed yourself to become involved in exploring the world that the playwright has created.

2. You must remember that you are writing about a *play*. At this stage this should seem so obvious that it hardly needs stating, but time and again examiners remark in their reports that candidates forget the stagecraft of the writer and the impact of the play on an audience. All your workshop activities and your exploration of the conventions and critical responses in relation to plays should ensure that you do not make this mistake.

3. Don't insult the examiner! It's not a good idea to suggest by the tone of your answer that you consider the examiner to be an idiot. In other words, your basic answer should not be 'This is a stupid question!' Questions are set and checked after lengthy deliberations but it is quite possible that any statements contained in them may well provoke you into strong disagreement. The question will put forward a reasoned viewpoint and you must counteract with cool argument any view with which you might differ.

Let's imagine that you have decided to answer the following question about Eliot's *Murder in the Cathedral*. It doesn't matter for the sake of our discussion if you don't know the play. I shall say sufficient to guide you through it.

'Who killed the Archbishop?' Comment on the effect and significance of the knights' speeches to the audience after the murder.

This question begins with a quotation from the play itself and it immediately points to the issue with which you are dealing. As it stands, the quotation suggests that there is some kind of mystery about the death of the Archbishop, but when you know the play you are aware that the murder of the Archbishop is carried out by the four knights in full view of the audience. Yet it is one of those knights who asks, 'Who killed the Archbishop?' When the knight asks that question he is obviously not asking precisely which knight struck the fatal blow; the question is asked for rhetorical effect and as a prelude to a number of speeches in which the knights address the audience directly, justifying their actions and insisting that not only was the Archbishop's death necessary but also that the audience, too, were in some way to blame. So, in a remarkable way, the key word in that quotation is *Who*, and I would underline it.

If you look carefully at the second half of the question, you can see that by underlining the two key issues on which you are asked to comment, there are really two questions:

Comment on the *effect* and *significance* of the knights' speeches to the audience after the murder.

Thus we could re-word what you are first asked to do, like this:

Bearing in mind the question of guilt for the Archbishop's death, comment on the *effect* of the knights' speeches to the audience after the murder.

You may also decide that remembering that this is a play designed to be performed, the words *to the audience* are particularly important because they point to something quite specific about the dramatist's stagecraft. The second question that I have identified by underlining a key word concerns the *significance* of the knights' speeches; that is not the same as the *effect*. You cannot hope to answer both questions at the same time.

The rule, then, is:

* Read the question very carefully and underline key words
* Create separate questions from the key words

Try this out on another question about the same play. It might be worth bearing in mind that at a recent conference of chief examiners the word 'Discuss' was taken to include 'Investigate or examine by argument; sift and debate; give reasons for and against; examine the implications'.

Discuss the role and presentation of the Chorus in *Murder in the Cathedral.*

Well, you should have underlined the words *role* and *presentation* to indicate the component questions, and possibly *Chorus* to remind yourself with whom you are dealing. You may ask, 'What's the point of all this? I can see I have to read the questions carefully, but why all this underlining?' The answer is, of course, that you don't just *read* the question: you *analyse* it. In order for you to see why this distinction is important, read this first paragraph from a student's answer to the question about 'Who killed the Archbishop?'

'Who killed the Archbishop?' is a quotation from one of the speeches of the four knights in *Murder in the Cathedral*. All four knights have very different characters and they each make a speech in which they explain why the Archbishop had to be killed. They end up by trying to make the audience feel guilty and then tell them to disperse quietly. Eliot said he wrote the play as an anti-nazi play and the four knights became like authorities in a police state who try to justify violence and say that it's necessary. One of the knights suspects that Thomas Becket was responsible for his own death.

I am sure you can sense that this has not begun very well. The student has some interesting things to say and has obviously read the play and something about it, but the answer already lacks any structure. The details of the question, the *effect* and the *significance*, have become confused and almost forgotten. Each sentence strikes out hopefully in a new direction without much reference to the previous sentence. The student seems to be looking for a way forward and every now and again feeds in a carefully learned fact in the hope of impressing the examiner. You will probably agree with me that the answer doesn't seem to be going anywhere and that there is no sense in which the student is mounting a well-considered argument. At the same time you may also feel that there is some merit in the fact that the quotation has been successfully identified and that the student obviously knows the incident to which the question refers.

However, had this student *analysed* the question, the response would have been so much better. The analysis will help you to shape your essay and that shape should be outlined in the *first paragraph*. A brief, clear statement of how you intend to tackle the answer is the best way to begin your response. You will remember that I underlined three key words. The first was in the quotation itself, which is *not* the real question but identifies an issue: '*Who* killed the Archbishop?' The two other words underlined are *effect* and *significance*, each of which identifies a different question. The plan for my essay ought to be that I first acknowledge the quotation as identifying a major issue in the play, then go on to show how the knights' speeches have an *effect*, and then discuss what significance they have when the question 'Who killed the Archbishop?' is posed. My opening paragraph might read as follows:

After the audience has watched the ritual killing of Becket in *Murder in the Cathedral* the knights suddenly turn to them and, addressing them directly, pose the question 'Who killed the Archbishop?' In this answer I intend to discuss the effect of this moment in the theatre when, for the second time, the audience is involved in the action of the play. I shall then go on to examine the significance of the knights' suggestion that the murder of Becket was necessary and inevitable and that the audience must share the guilt.

You can see that I have already decided on the two main parts of my essay and have thought clearly about the word *effect*, so that I realise that it has to do with the performance of the play. I indicate that Eliot has already used this technique once, and this will enable me to make comparisons in the following paragraphs. I have also said something about the nature of Becket's death: I have described it as a 'ritual killing', and this will help me to explain the effect of the very different kind of action that follows it. I have given enough pointers for me to pick up in subsequent paragraphs. I have also revealed that I have spotted the difference between the *effect* that happens in a moment in time and the *significance* that concerns the themes and issues of the play. So you can see that although this opening paragraph is brief it says enough to set up the rest of my essay and help me to organise my thoughts.

My *second paragraph* might begin something like this:

The effect of the knights' speeches on the audience is one of shock, because the speeches are totally unexpected. During the murder of Becket the knights have enacted a ritual created by their own doggerel verse and the great lament of the Chorus. Now, however, the nature of the action suddenly changes and becomes realistic. The language also changes from verse to colloquial prose, so the experience of the audience moves from witnessing a remote historical event to being directly confronted by the implications of the action. Eliot has in some ways prepared the audience for this moment by his use of direct address in Becket's sermon, that also has a bearing on the question of 'Who killed the Archbishop?'

You will see that this is a simple paragraph consisting of three elements. First there is my *statement* 'The effect of the knights' speeches on the audience is one of shock', to which I have added a reinforcing statement, that the 'speeches are totally unexpected'. It's important to begin with a clear, unambiguous statement that says exactly what you want it to say, and there is no doubt that I've made a bold assertion here. Now I must *justify* what I have said, so the next element in my paragraph is a section of *evidence* that explains why the knights' speeches have the effect they do. This is the part of my answer where I demonstrate that I have understood and recognised the different codes of communication being employed by the playwright. I have chosen to concentrate at this point on change – change from ritual to realism, change from verse to prose and change from detached spectator to involved participant; in other words I have drawn upon my understanding of the conventions operating in the play and *specific examples from the play* to show why this moment constitutes a theatrical shock. By using these examples I have engaged in a brief *discussion* of the topic. The examples are meaningless unless I *do* offer some discussion, and in this instance what I have done is to take the idea of shock brought about by sudden change and then pointed to different kinds of change to which the audience is subjected. My penultimate sentence also offers a *conclusion* to this very short section of the argument. I have moved from saying that the initial effect is a shock to the fact that this has a further effect – that of making the audience feel involved in a contemporary issue. Finally, taking the central idea of the paragraph, I have moved towards another point in the argument in a *linking* statement that naturally leads me on to a further paragraph.

In that *third paragraph* I should examine Becket's sermon in the play and its effect. It consists of a speech directed straight at the audience as if they were members of the cast. Then I should briefly explain *how* that speech contrasts with the knights' speeches and how that contrast adds to the sense of shock and emphasises the question of the Archbishop's death. I should then be ready to move into a *fourth paragraph*, which would begin to examine more fully the individual speeches of the knights, always remembering it is their *effect* that is my chief concern.

Successful paragraphing is really the key to essay writing and your paragraphs should lead naturally from one to another. As the essay progresses you must take straightforward, honest statements about your response to the play and develop the argument you want to make as a reasoned answer to the question. A paragraph is simply a unit of thought in which you make statements and justify them in a logical sequence. Many of your paragraphs will be of the simple kind I have just described, but you may need to deal with rather more complex issues that demand an extension of this simple form. This would be quite likely when it came to dealing with the *second part* of our sample question, the part that asks about the *significance* of the knights' speeches. Let's suppose that I have decided that the final speech of the First Knight, which includes a suggestion to 'disperse quietly' and a thinly veiled threat, is confirmation that Eliot is portraying elements of a police state. I also want to link this to the fact that loyalty to the state has been an issue throughout the play. This is an altogether more complicated affair than the simple paragraph can accommodate; so the paragraph discussing this aspect of the subject may need to be quite long and will need to contain several sets of evidence and comment before moving to a conclusion. So the shape of my paragraph will be as follows:

- A statement about the idea of a police state
- Various pieces of evidence from the play – perhaps confined to the knights' speeches
- Discussion of this evidence
- More evidence, that uses other parts of the play
- Discussion of this set of evidence
- Conclusion that draws together both discussions
- Link to the next paragraph

You will notice that in my example I have assumed that I can quote the final speech of the First Knight accurately: this is because in my earlier study of the play I would have identified it as a *key* speech.

I shall now summarise the whole process from the moment of reading the question before I add a few extra words of advice. You must proceed step-by-step as follows:

1. Read the question carefully, underlining important words and phrases.
2. Form a number of questions out of these key words.
3. Decide what statements you want to make about the play in relation to the questions.
4. Select the examples you will use as evidence to back up your statements.
5. Decide on a logical order for the statements and paragraphs.
6. Write a simple opening paragraph briefly outlining your intentions for the essay.
7. Present your argument in uncluttered, unpretentious language structured in paragraphs. Each paragraph should also be clearly structured, move to a conclusion, and link to the next paragraph. The last paragraph should briefly and clearly summarise the conclusions of your essay.

You may remember that I said earlier that there are various kinds of question that occur in exams and I have given you some examples. You should supplement this by looking at examples of questions set on your particular play from past papers. This is a good idea in itself but it also highlights the whole question of *relevance*. If I am asked a question about verbal communication in *Waiting for Godot* it's no earthly good my writing about visual symbolism because I happen to have revised that topic specially in the hope that it might come up. Nor is it any good my thinking, 'Ah, this is really the same question as the one they set last year', and then reeling off my carefully prepared answer. You must *read* and *answer* the question in front of you – no two questions are *ever* the same, and you must be prepared to apply your knowledge and understanding of the play in the way required of you.

To conclude, I shall now turn my attention to the kind of question that involves reading an extract from a play you have studied and commenting on it. Your first and main task is to *identify precisely what is being asked of you* in relation to the extract. As we have seen, a dramatic text yields up many kinds of information, and if you write down everything that occurs to you, you are going to end up with an excessively long answer that is nothing more than a hotch-potch of ideas. On the other hand, you now realise that the words, the stage directions, the conventions, the action and the activities are all codes of communication that are partners in creating a stage image; so you must use your practised eye in reading the text. The secret of answering such questions well is to keep the precise question in mind as you confront the extract, and gradually to narrow down the attention you give to both, as follows:

1. Read the question through carefully, but don't linger over it, just get a clear sense of what it is asking you to do.
2. Read through the extract fairly quickly and try to establish its context in the play. Pause for a few minutes to think where it fits into the action of the play and imagine the action happening in front of you. You ought to be able to pick up the importance of the particular event selected at this stage.
3. Go back to the question and analyse it. Treat it as we did before and especially underline the key words and phrases that tell you what you are looking for.
4. Comb the extract for evidence of the issue you are discussing. Take your time over this.
5. Think how this evidence relates to the rest of the play.
6. Structure your answer as a brief essay arranged in a series of paragraphs of roughly the same length. Plan your answer in this way and you will avoid giving the impression that you are simply jotting down all you know. Instead, try to construct a sensible, logical analysis of the extract.

All the rules for clear, logical writing apply here too and you must demonstrate that you are able to draw from the given passage all the evidence needed to justify the points you make. Every part of the process of learning I have commended to you in this book will be relevant to this task. But what will also be relevant, and what I hope you have gained from this book, is a keen sense of and interest in modern drama both as playtext and performance.

Checklist

Key topics covered in this chapter:

- The concept of 'character' in a play
- Themes and issues of a play
- Analysing essay or examination questions
- Recognising various parts of a question
- Constructing a clear, logical response to any exam or essay question
- Responding to a given piece of dramatic text with insight and clarity

---

▶ **Suggested activities**

1. Take any four speeches from *Death of a Salesman* and analyse them to decide what attitudes are being expressed by the characters. Refer to other parts of the play that might have influenced your views of these characters.

2. Select a long speech from a play you have been studying and analyse it using the six steps I have introduced to you in the final section of this chapter.

3. Select a question from a past examination paper dealing with a play that you know and plan your answer using the seven steps I have outlined in this chapter.

Suggestions for Further Study

▶ Study skills

If you feel that you need further help in your own personal approach to study you can turn to Palgrave Macmillan's website *www.skills4study.com*. More help in applying those skills to drama can be found in *Thinking About Plays* (Dramatic Lines) by Giles Auckland-Lewis and Kenneth Pickering (2003); *Reading Drama* (Hodder & Stoughton) by Richard Griffiths (2001) or *The Drama Handbook* (Oxford) by John Lennard and Mary Luckhurst (2002).

▶ Plays

It is important to use good, accurate editions of your set plays: editions published by Methuen, Faber & Faber, Penguin, Oberon and Nick Hern Books are very reliable. This last publisher is particularly helpful in publishing the latest plays to have been performed. Many of these editions have helpful introductory notes, but rather more extensive notes and commentary are provided in the *Methuen Student Editions* and the *Hereford Plays* from Heinemann. Any comments by the playwrights are particularly useful, but, like editors' notes, these should only be used to extend your interest in the play and not as a substitute for your personal engagement with the text. Fortunately there is now a very efficient system whereby new plays appear in print very quickly and you should visit theatre bookshops whenever you can.

▶ Playwrights

Once you have studied a play you will certainly find it useful to read something about the playwright and his or her work. There are a number of good critical accounts of the work of individual playwrights and of these the *Modern Theatre Profile* series from Methuen, *The Modern Dramatists* series from Palgrave Macmillan and the *Contemporary Playwrights* series from Heinemann are all very readable. Particularly interesting insights into the way that modern playwrights go about their work can be gained from *Making Plays* (Palgrave Macmillan) by Duncan Wu, *State of Play* (Faber & Faber) edited by David Edgar, *The Royal Court Theatre and the Modern Stage* (CUP) by Philip Roberts, and *How Good is David Mamet, Anyway?* (Routledge) by John Heilpern. There are many fascinating books about Ibsen, the father of modern drama; you would find *Ibsen: The Dramaturgy of Fear* (Columbia UP) by Michael Goldman particularly stimulating.

▶ Overviews

It is often very helpful to consult a single volume dealing with modern drama as an entity. You might well start with Stephen Unwin and Carole Woddis's *A Pocket Guide to Twentieth Century Drama* or Michelene Wandor's *A Critical Guide to British Drama 1970–1990*, but there is a superb account of the development of the British theatre in the twentieth century in *Changing Stages* (Bloomsbury) by Richard Eyre and Nicholas Wright. Both Methuen and Nick Hern publish excellent collections of plays drawn from certain periods, and these, too, provide a real sense of the context in which the plays were written. A good example is *The Methuen Book of Sixties Drama*.

▶ Theory and criticism

Eric Bentley's *The Theory of the Modern Stage* (Penguin) and Martin Esslin's *The Theatre of the Absurd* (Methuen) remain classic accounts of significant movements in modern drama. In order to acquire a rich vocabulary with which to discuss modern drama you will find considerable assistance in *Literary Terms and Criticism* (Palgrave Macmillan) by John Peck and Martin Coyle. *Modern Theories of Performance* by Jane Milling and Graham Ley (Palgrave Macmillan) or *The Death of the Playwright: Modern British Drama and Literary Theory* edited by Adrian Page (Palgrave Macmillan) will enable you to come to grips with various new approaches to the criticism of drama. A very stimulating view of the role of theatre in society can be obtained from John McGrath's *A Good Night Out* (Nick Hern) and there is an excellent opportunity to read the work of Britain's finest theatre critic, Michael Billington, in his book *One Night Stands* (Nick Hern). If you are interested in the issue of gender and sexual politics in drama, you will find *Gender and Genre: Essays on David Mamet* (Palgrave Macmillan) edited by Hudgins and Kane, *An Introduction to Feminism and Theatre* (Routledge) by Elaine Aston, and *Staging Gay Lives* (Westview Press) edited by John Clum all very useful. Finally I should mention some of the great classics of modern theatre theory: *Brecht* on *Art and Politics* (Methuen) edited by Kuhn and Giles, Brecht's *Messingkauf Dialogues* (Methuen) edited by John Willett, Peter Brook's *The Empty Space* (Penguin), Boal's *Theatre of the Oppressed* (Pluto), and Grotowski's *Towards a Poor Theatre* (Methuen).

▶ Workshop approaches

Tutors and students will find general help to this approach in Kenneth Pickering's *Drama Improvised* (Garnet Miller), while there is extensive help in the process of devising activities in *Devising Theatre: A Practical and Theoretical Handbook* (Routledge) by Alison Oddey, and *Devising: A Handbook for Drama and Theatre Studies* (Hodder & Stoughton) by Gill Lamden.

Supplementary List of Suggested Plays for Study

▶ The late nineteenth century and early twentieth

Henrik Ibsen, *The Master Builder* (1892) and *The Pillars of Society* (1877)
August Strindberg, *The Father* (1887)
Anton Chekhov, *The Seagull* (1896) and *The Three Sisters* (1901)
J. M. Barrie, *The Twelve-Pound Look* (1910)
Luigi Pirandello, *Six Characters in search of an Author* (1921)
G. B. Shaw, *Pygmalion* (1912)
Noel Coward, *Private Lives* (1930)
T. S. Eliot, *The Family Reunion* (1939)
Ernst Toller, *Masses and Man* (1921)

▶ The 1940s

Eugene O'Neill, *A Long Day's Journey into Night* (1939–41)
Arthur Miller, *All My Sons* (1947)
Terence Rattigan, *The Winslow Boy* (1946)
Tennessee Williams, *A Streetcar Named Desire* (1947)
Jean Genet, *The Maids* (1947)
Berthold Brecht, *The Good Person of Setzuan* (1940)

▶ The 1950s

Shelagh Delaney, *A Taste of Honey* (1958)
Eugene Ionesco, *The Bald Prima Donna* (1950)
Brendan Behan, *The Hostage* (1958)
Arnold Wesker, *The Kitchen* (1958)
Ann Jellicoe, *The Sport of My Mad Mother* (1957)
Edward Albee, *Zoo Story* (1958)

▶ The 1960s

John Osborne, *Luther* (1961)
John Whiting, *The Devils* (1960)
Theatre Workshop, *Oh What a Lovely War* (1963)
Peter Shaffer, *The Royal Hunt of the Sun* (1964)
Peter Nichols, *The National Health* (1969)
Harold Pinter, *Landscape* (1967) and *Silence* (1968)

▶ The 1970s

David Storey, *The Changing Room* (1971)
David Hare, *Plenty* (1978)
Howard Brenton, *Epsom Downs* (1977)
Edward Bond, *The Sea* (1973)
Tom Stoppard, *Jumpers* (1972)
Stephen Poliakoff, *City Sugar* (1976)

▶ The 1980s

Louise Page, *Golden Girls* (1982)
David Edgar, *Maydays* (1980)
Caryl Churchill, *Top Girls* (1982)
Sharmon McDonald, *When I Was a Girl I Used to Scream and Shout* (1984)
Winsome Pinnock, *A Hero's Welcome* (1989)

▶ The 1990s

Pam Gems, *Deborah's Daughter* (1994)
David Lan, *Desire* (1995)
Ayub Khan-Din, *East is East* (1994)
Patrick Marber, *Dealer's Choice* (1996)
Sam Shepard, *Simpatico* (1996)
Sarah Kane, *Phaedra's Love* (1998)

▶ The twenty-first century

Enda Walsh, *Bedbound* (2000)
Amanda Whittington, *Be My Baby* (2000)
Tony Kushner, *Homebody/Kabul* (2002)
Owen McCafferty, *Closing Time* (2002)
Conor McPherson, *Dublin Carol* (2003)
August Wilson, *Jitney* (2002)

Index

ASFC LEARNING CENTRE